W9-CPE-287

TERRY DUNNAHOO

PEARL HARBOR

AMERICA ENTERS THE WAR

FOREWORD BY
JESSE E. POND, JR.

Barbara Silberdick Feinberg,
Consulting Editor

FRANKLIN WATTS
A TWENTIETH CENTURY
AMERICAN HISTORY BOOK
NEW YORK LONDON TORONTO
SYDNEY 1991

Library of Congress Cataloging-in-Publication Data

Dunnahoo, Terry.
    Pearl Harbor : America enters the war / Terry Dunnahoo.
       p.   cm. — (A Twentieth century American history book)
    Includes bibliographical references and index.
    Summary: Discusses the buildup of the Japanese military, the move
of America's Pacific fleet to Hawaii, and relations between the two
nations prior to the attack on Pearl Harbor, which drew the United
States into World War II.
    ISBN 0-531-11010-9
    1. Pearl Harbor (Hawaii), Attack on, 1941—Juvenile literature.
[1. Pearl Harbor (Hawaii), Attack on, 1941. 2. World War,
1939–1945—Causes. 3. Japan—Foreign relations—United States.
4. United States—Foreign relations—Japan.] I. Title. II. Series.
D767.92.D86   1991
940.54'26—dc20   90-13035   CIP   AC

To my niece, Geraldine,
with love

CONTENTS

FOREWORD

December 7, 1941, "a date which will live in infamy," was not an isolated, spur-of-the-moment event, but the result of a slow, inexorable process.

As someone who actively participated in the defense against the attack, I was witness to the great destruction and havoc wrought in those 110 minutes. If the words of the philosopher Santayana are true—that "those who cannot remember the past are condemned to repeat it"—then it is important that young Americans know about the actions that led to Pearl Harbor and learn from that experience.

War between the United States and the empire of Japan was not inevitable. But given the mind-set of the cultures involved, conflict seemed unavoidable. At the 1905 Treaty of Portsmouth in New Hampshire, President Theodore Roosevelt negotiated the settlement of the Russo-Japanese War. The Japanese delegates returned home humiliated by the treaty's terms. They felt that the mediators had been more sympathetic to the Russian diplomats than to them, and that the American press had ridiculed them. Again, at the 1923 Washington and the 1930 London naval treaty negotiations, Japan felt it was given second-class status.

The Japanese were a proud people who lived in a closed society, a society with little contact with the outside world. Isoroku Yamamoto had spent many months in the United States and admired the country and the people, but he completely misread the American mind. When Japan decided to wage war on the United States, preparations started long before Yamamoto devised his plan to strike Pearl Harbor. Yamamoto felt that if he eliminated the U.S. Pacific fleet in one hard, swift blow, the Americans would not fight. If they did not quit there and then, he said, he would run wild for six months, and then the United States' great industrial might would win out.

The American high command also misread the Japanese mind. Anglo-Saxon racism ran high, as public statements such as "The Japanese can't fly airplanes—their eyes are no good," "We'd wipe out their navy in two weeks," and "Those little yellow so-and-sos know better than to attack us" appeared in the U.S. press. In truth the Japanese had good ships, good planes, and a well-trained and experienced naval force. They had beaten the Russians handily, they had conquered Manchuria and Korea with ease, and they believed that they were God's chosen people and feared no one.

In the late 1930s, the United States was just emerging out of the Great Depression and there were many diverse groups in the news. One such group was the isolationists, who shunned foreign entanglements. When World War II broke out, the war in Europe was something that most Americans feared and wanted to avoid at all costs. While campaigning for his third term of office, Franklin D. Roosevelt promised not to send American boys overseas.

The country was politically divided, pulled and tugged in every direction. However, if the Japanese had tried, they could not have better succeeded in uniting our nation than by attacking it without warning on a Sunday morning. The sea-and-air raid of December 7, 1941, was a great tactical success, but a strategic error of the first magnitude. America rose as one man to "remember Pearl Harbor."

The Pearl Harbor attack ended America's undercover attempts to aid England and swept us into the war with both feet. Great Britain was having a very hard time fighting Hitler (there was grave doubt that the British would survive), but with the United States' open involvement, Great Britain could view its future with optimism.

There have been books written about Pearl Harbor that have blamed our leadership and presented theories about broken codes and collusion in high places to get us into the war. At that time there was no Central Intelligence Agency to gather all the bits of intelligence and to winnow out nuggets of useful information. Each service—the Navy, the Army, and the Federal Bureau of Investigation—had its own intelligence-gathering group, and they did not, or would not, share information with one another.

There were turf wars among these groups where people jealously guarded their fiefdoms. There were "tons" of data coming into these units to be translated, decoded, and passed on to superiors for evaluation and action. With such a bureaucratic setup, made worse by the chronic shortage of manpower in every intelligence group, it is surprising that any useful information was gathered and used.

The Japanese planned the strike carefully and painstakingly, and they were blessed by Lady Luck every step of the way. Jingoism (an arrogant form of nationalism marked by a warlike foreign policy) had been raised to an art form in Japan. Assassination threats against individuals or groups with pro-Western leanings permeated Japanese politics. And the young Japanese officers' belief in their abilities matched up with the racism in America to make conflict inevitable.

The Pacific war started with the destruction of a single fleet. It escalated from one increasingly bloody island invasion to another, climaxing in the carnage in Okinawa, when the kamikazes struck the fleet offshore and assault troops suffered a 35 percent casualty rate. It soon became obvious that any invasion of the Japanese-held islands would be a formidable task.

Planning for Operation Downfall involved a two-pronged assault. One, code-named Olympic, was scheduled to hit Kyushu, Japan, in the fall of 1945. The second mission, Coronet, was scheduled to land on Honshu the following spring. Olympic alone called for 767,000 U.S. troops. Using statistics taken from the Okinawa clashes, this meant that there would be 268,000 American ground casualties alone. This number did not take into account the casualties that could result had the invading fleet been hit by the thousands of kamikazes that Japan had been accumulating to repel the invasion.

The first estimate of Japanese casualties for Olympic was set at over 2 million. But the Japanese had said that they would fight down to the last man, woman, and child. It is my opinion, borne out by postwar Japanese estimates of their own war losses, that the losses to Japanese civilians would have surpassed 25 million.

Knowing our feelings at the time, and having come out of the experience of Okinawa, I am sure that we would have wiped out the Japanese nation. I think that American losses would have swelled into the millions as well. The few hundred thousand who died in Hiroshima and Nagasaki as a result of the use of atomic weapons did not die in vain. The quick ending of the war ultimately saved millions of lives, lives that went on to build and rebuild both nations.

—JESSE E. POND, JR.

DEATH AND DESTRUCTION

Sunday in Honolulu, Hawaii, was for sleeping in, eating pancakes, going to church, reading the comics, lying on the beach, having a picnic, shopping, and hanging around. The people who lived on the beautiful island of Oahu thought December 7, 1941, would be the same as any other Sunday. They hardly paid attention to the hum of the planes in the distance. When the hum came closer and turned into a roar, most people believed the planes were part of a U.S. Navy or Army drill.

An officer of the deck on the light cruiser *Raleigh* also thought he was watching a drill, until a torpedo hit the water and blasted into his ship. The *Utah*, which was moored beside the *Raleigh*, also took a hit. The officer sounded the attack alarm.

A plane dove over a general's house at Schofield Barracks. The general raced to the window to try to see the number on the wings. The number could tell the general who was flying the plane. Whoever it was, the general thought, he was going to be in real trouble for low-flying over Schofield. But the general did not see a number. He saw red emblems representing the rising sun. It was a Japanese plane.

The plane pulled out of the dive and flew over the

minelayer *Oglala*, a ship equipped to lay explosive mines in the water. When its commander saw the rising sun emblems, he raised the alert flag to warn ships of an enemy attack. The time was 7:55 A.M. Before his sailors could reach their guns, a torpedo passed under the *Oglala* and hit the *Helena*. The ship's clock stopped at 7:57. The torpedo exploded between the two vessels and damaged both.

On the battleship *Nevada*, band members waited on the afterdeck to play "The Star-Spangled Banner" during the ship's flag raising. The sailors saw planes swoop over the navy's airfield on Ford Island, pull out of their dives, and head for U.S. ships grouped together like sitting ducks. At 8, the band started "The Star-Spangled Banner," and the flag rose. The sailors braved bullets until they finished playing. Then they ran for their lives. Later, the leader explained that when the band played "The Star-Spangled Banner," it was customary to play until the last note sounded.

Battleships All in a Row

Ensign Joseph K. Taussig, Jr., on the *Nevada* pulled the alarm bell at 8:01. Then he took charge of his battle station. A moment later, his men were firing their ship's guns. One Japanese plane fell. By the time they hit a second plane, its torpedo was streaking toward the *Nevada*. At 8:03 the torpedo tore a hole in the ship. Debris from the explosion passed through Ensign Taussig's thigh. A pharmacist's mate bandaged the wound, and Taussig stayed on deck to direct the battle from a stretcher.

By now the *Oklahoma*, the *West Virginia*, and the *Arizona* had been hit. On the *Oklahoma* the water level rose in the living and working areas, and the emergency lights went out. Giant gun shells broke loose and rumbled across the floor, knocking over sailors as if they were bowling pins. Water was pouring in through holes in the ship's side as the sailors scrambled to their feet.

Some escaped through the ventilation system and portholes. Others tried to escape up ladders. But with pandemonium breaking loose, many of the ladders were blocked. Sailors pushed their way toward the top decks. Few made it. Explosions on deck drove the sailors back, and they fell on others trying to get up. Movement stopped. More than four hundred sailors were trapped under water inside the Oklahoma. They swam through the darkness searching for air pockets and prayed for help.

Some sailors above deck dove into the water. Others walked with the roll of the ship, and when the rails reached the water, they swam. Their waterlogged clothes dragged them down, and oil-coated water burned all around them. Some survived, but many did not. Three brothers did; one brother's watch stopped when he hit the water at 8:10. Survivors from the Oklahoma climbed aboard other ships and used the ships' guns to try to stop the Japanese planes.

Moments after the Oklahoma rolled over, the Arizona exploded and sent up mountains of fire and smoke. The shock wave created by the explosion knocked sailors off the Vestal, the Nevada, and the West Virginia. The explosion scattered bodies and limbs everywhere. More than a thousand sailors died at that moment, including an admiral and every member of the ship's band gathered to play "The Star-Spangled Banner" for the Arizona's flag raising. Sailors trapped inside the ship crammed clothes, mattresses, sheets, and towels into cracks to keep out smoke. In other parts of the ship men wrapped themselves in blankets to protect themselves from the fire that surrounded them.

ABANDON SHIP. The order came loud and clear, and sailors jumped into the water blackened with oil oozing from damaged ships. Some swam past arms, legs, heads, and other body parts to shore or to other ships. A few men grabbed a rope tossed from the repair ship *Vestal*, docked alongside the *Arizona*. They inched themselves aboard while the *Vestal's* crew pulled burned sailors from the water. Most died moments later.

Earlier, the *Vestal* had been hit by a bomb that set it on fire. But the explosion on the *Arizona* was so powerful it acted the way a candle snuffer puts out a flame. It pulled the oxygen from the *Vestal's* fires and saved the ship. Without oxygen, fire cannot burn.

The explosion on the *Arizona* blew the *Vestal's* captain and about a hundred of its sailors overboard. With its captain gone and with water flooding through holes into the ship, an officer ordered the crew to abandon ship. But before most of them could leave, the oil-soaked captain climbed out of the water and ordered his men back aboard. Most of them obeyed, and the commander gave orders to cast off. Sailors cut the lines that tied the *Vestal* to what was left of the *Arizona*, and a navy tug towed it away from the blazing ship.

Debris from the *Arizona* tore through the bridge of the *West Virginia*, wounding its captain. His men moved him to a safer place, and when flames and smoke filled the ship, he told the pharmacist who had bandaged his wounds to leave and save himself. The pharmacist stayed. After the captain died, the pharmacist manned a machine gun to fight off the Japanese planes. But the gun was useless against the enemy. After the fires on the *West Virginia* became more life-threatening, sailors escaped to the *Tennessee* by using its guns as bridges to cross over the burning water.

A torpedo hit the *California* at 8:05. A second torpedo followed, and water poured in. When the electricity went out and shells from the ammunition room could not move to the guns automatically, sailors passed the shells by hand. Many fainted from heat and exhaustion, and others took their places. While these people worked to keep the guns firing, rescue parties tried to save trapped sailors. And others worked to keep the ship afloat, despite the fire and smoke.

The *Maryland* caught only two bombs. The ship was moored inboard of the *Oklahoma*, which protected the *Maryland* from torpedoes. Because of the ship's position, many sailors who had escaped from other ships climbed to safety aboard the *Maryland*.

Hickam Field

At Hickam Field, the Army Air Corps base, bombers had been lined up wing-tip to wing-tip to make it easier to guard them against sabotage. Moments past 8 o'clock, a Japanese plane swooped over the field and dropped a bomb. Seconds later, more planes strafed the ground from treetop level. Bullets and bombs hit the mess hall, hangars, offices, and barracks. Many of the people racing for cover fell, their bodies riddled with bullets.

While enemy planes attacked Hickam, a dozen U.S. B-17s were coming in over the field. The planes had been flying from San Francisco for fourteen hours, and their crews looked forward to breakfast and sleep. Instead of a safe landing strip, the pilots saw rows of American planes burning below them and planes with the rising sun emblems on their wings flying above them, under them, beside them, and behind them. For a split second a couple of pilots, who did not see the rising sun emblem right away, thought the planes were a welcoming committee. But the chatter of guns changed their minds.

The B-17s had no guns to defend themselves. When they left San Francisco the day before, their ammunition was taken out to lighten the planes. This was done to save gas so that the B-17s could reach Hickam before their tanks were empty. Even with the planes stripped, their gauges had hovered on "empty" as they approached Hawaii. Now the crews not only worried about landing before their planes ran out of gas, they worried about getting killed by enemy guns.

Some of the B-17s landed at Hickam around 8:20. As soon as they touched down, their crews ran for cover. While they hugged the ground, Hickam's fire fighters worked to put out fires that sprouted everywhere, but many of the water mains had been shattered by bombs. Moments later, Japanese planes ended any hope of putting out the fires. Explosions blasted the fire station to the ground, injuring or killing most of the fire fighters.

With the injured and dead lying everywhere and buildings and planes burning, fear and panic turned to anger. Soldiers aimed machine guns at Japanese planes. But the planes flew off to other targets. Their pilots were not afraid of the return fire. Machine guns could do little damage to their planes. They left because, within minutes, they had hit all of their targets.

The B-17 pilots who could not land at Hickam tried to land at Wheeler Field or Ewa Field. But there were so many fires below them, the pilots flew instead to Haleiwa Airfield on the west coast of Oahu. They came down safely on a strip built for small planes, not B-17s.

Schofield Barracks

When Japanese planes began diving over Schofield Barracks, the breakfast chow line was winding through the quads. Some soldiers ran for cover, but others did not want to leave their places in the chow line. Then the planes opened fire, and people scrambled for their lives.

The planes were so low that Sergeant Henry Raymond Mullaney saw the faces of the Japanese, their goggles glistening in the sun. He dodged their bullets to get to the gun supply room, his dog running beside him. Bullets rained around them. Mullaney was not hit, but his dog fell dead, a bullet in its side. Mullaney hesitated then ran for a gun to defend the barracks. He found the guns locked up and a sign on the door warning that ammunition could not be given out without orders from an officer. Orders were orders. But lives were lives. Soldiers kicked down the door, grabbed guns, and began shooting.

Wheeler Field

Like the planes at Hickam, the army planes at Wheeler were lined up wing-tip to wing-tip to protect them from sabotage. At 8:02 a guard saw bombers coming toward the field and recognized the rising sun emblems on the wings. He dropped his rifle and ran for a machine gun. The shack was locked, and he could not get at the guns. At Wheeler, twenty-five bombers dropped their bombs on planes and hangars with hardly any return fire from the ground. The Japanese hit everything—planes, hangars, the post exchange, even the golf course. One bomb hit a barracks, wounding and killing hundreds. Then the planes circled back to strafe soldiers running to help the wounded or trying to get guns or save what planes they could.

Saving planes was a losing battle. Each plane that was hit set the one next to it on fire. Planes blew up in a chain reaction while soldiers broke locks on the ammunition shacks and set up guns. But it was too little too late. Although the Japanese planes came back several times to strafe the area, no enemy plane was hit over Wheeler.

Lieutenants Kenneth Taylor and George Welch were at Wheeler that morning. They were stationed at Haleiwa and had come to Wheeler for the Saturday night dance. They stayed on to play cards. Now they saw planes burning at Wheeler Field and called Haleiwa to ask if their planes were all right. They were, and Taylor and Welch ordered them gassed and loaded with ammunition. Then they hopped into Taylor's car and, dodging bullets, headed for Haleiwa.

When they got there, their planes were gassed up, but they were not fully loaded with ammunition. Anxious to get into the action, they took off anyway. During the next hour they landed at Wheeler for more ammunition, found themselves surrounded by Japanese planes and shot down a couple; then they went to Ewa and shot down more. Taylor was forced to land with a bullet wound in his arm. Welch kept flying. The Japanese lost twenty-nine planes during their attack on Pearl Harbor. Taylor and Welch were credited with shooting down seven of them.

By the time Taylor and Welch landed for the day, every ship in Battleship Row had been damaged. Every ship had its cowards and heroes. Each had its wounded and its dead. And the smells and sounds of death and destruction were everywhere.

2

TORA! TORA! TORA!

Flying high above the destruction, the Japanese were happy to see that their planning and training were paying off. They had worked for months for this moment, and in a few minutes they had crippled the U.S. Pacific Fleet.

The planes had flown to Pearl Harbor from six aircraft carriers that were still waiting for them about 200 miles (320 km) north of Oahu. Before the men climbed into their planes that morning, they ate *sekihan*, rice boiled with tiny red beans. Japanese eat *sekihan* before special occasions, and the attack on Pearl Harbor was a most special occasion. The men also drank sake, the Japanese rice wine, and prayed at shrines set up on each ship.

At 5:30 A.M. two seaplanes took off from the carriers to scout the route to Pearl Harbor. If American planes or ships spotted them, they would be shot down, and the pilots would probably die. But they were ready to die. So were the more than three hundred pilots and their crews who had been chosen to take part in the attack. The Japanese forces lived by a code of honor, and the men had decided that if their planes had engine trouble, they would deliberately crash into U.S. ships and destroy them for their emperor. They would rather die in glory for Emperor Hirohito than live in disgrace as American prisoners of war.

The men had prepared for death in different ways. Most wrote farewell letters to their mothers, fathers, wives, and children. In keeping with a Japanese rite, one man put a lock of hair and his fingernail clippings in a letter to his loved ones. One prayed to live so that he could watch his baby daughter grow up. Another put on perfume so that he could die smelling like cherry blossoms falling to the ground.

Before the planes took off, the men were given *hachimakis*, with the word *Hissho* written on them, to tie around their heads. The word meant "certain victory." People who wore *hachimakis* told the world that they were ready to die for their country. Commander Mitsuo Fuchida, leader of the First Air Fleet, received a special white *hachimaki*. He tied the scarf around his helmet and climbed aboard his plane.

Fuchida also wore red underwear and a red shirt. He had decided that if he were hit by enemy bullets his blood would mix with the red of his underwear and shirt and his men would not see the blood. He worried that if they saw their leader had been wounded, they might concentrate on him instead of on their jobs.

The First Air Fleet Takes Off

Despite the threat of death the men were anxious to take part in Operation Hawaii, which is what the Japanese called the attack on Pearl Harbor. They had waited impatiently beside their planes on the decks of the carriers while weather and rough seas delayed takeoff for twenty minutes. But when they finally received the signal to go, the launching of the first group of planes took only fifteen minutes.

Fighter planes flew off first so that they could protect

the torpedo planes and bombers. Fuchida's bomber had three seats, the rising sun emblem on its wings, red and yellow stripes on the tail, and a bomb under its belly. As leader, Fuchida would direct his men using hand signals. Radio contact between planes would alert Americans of unidentified aircraft in the area.

Of the 185 planes in the first group, one crashed into the water, and the pilot was picked up by one of the ships. The second plane had engine trouble and did not get off the carrier's deck. Finally, Fuchida's group of planes was on its way to Pearl Harbor at around 6:20. It would take more than an hour to reach its targets.

As soon as the first group of planes had left, the carrier crews raised the second group on elevators from their hangars below decks. Only one plane, which had engine trouble, was left behind in the second group. Altogether, 350 planes headed for Oahu. The deck crews cheered and waved their caps, with tears of joy running down their faces. They did not stop waving until the planes were out of sight.

As Fuchida's planes flew in formation, he did not know how many planes from the second group had made it off the carriers. And he did not have much time to think about it. Clouds hid the ground from him, and he worried that he might fly over Pearl Harbor and have to backtrack. This would throw him off schedule, and he would miss his chance for a surprise attack.

To check his course, he turned the radio dial until he found KGMB, one of Honolulu's radio stations. By using the station's beam, he learned that he was five degrees off course, and his pilot made the correction. So did the other planes. Fuchida listened for interruptions in the music. But the music did not stop. If Americans suspected an attack, he would hear warnings, not love songs.

Enemy Planes and Submarines

Fuchida would have been more worried if he had known that soldiers at the Opana Mobile Radar Station had seen his planes on their radar screens at 7:02. The soldiers' job was to report sightings on the radar screens to the Combat Information Center at Fort Shafter, about 30 miles (51 km) south of the Opana Station.

Because the U.S. Army thought that if an attack came it would come between 4 A.M. and 7 A.M., the station was open only during those hours. The two privates at Opana were getting ready to shut down when they saw so many blips on the screens that they thought something was wrong with their equipment.

They worked the dials to check their sets, unable to believe so many planes could be heading for Hawaii. The soldiers talked about calling Fort Shafter and then decided against it. It was after 7, and they were off duty. But another look at the screens convinced them that the sighting had to be reported.

The lieutenant in charge at Fort Shafter listened to the privates' report. After discussing it, the lieutenant decided that the planes on the radar screen were B-17s coming in from San Francisco. He told the privates to close down the radar. But they were so fascinated by what they saw that they kept watching. At 7:20 the screens showed Fuchida's planes 74 miles (118 km) away. At 7:39, they were 20 miles (32 km) away.

As his plane got closer to Oahu, Fuchida could not believe his good luck. He saw no American planes in the air and no gunfire from the ground. And he was still hearing love songs instead of attack warnings from KGMB. What he did not know was that his crews would soon see B-17s coming in from California. Like Fuchida, these planes were using KGMB to guide them to Hawaii.

Fuchida also did not know that two of his countrymen had already died for Operation Hawaii. Shortly before 4 that morning, a U.S. naval officer on the minesweeper *Condor* had flashed its signal lights to the destroyer *Ward*. The signal reported a submarine heading for the entrance to Pearl Harbor.

Searching for submarines was one of the *Ward's* jobs, and the officer on duty looked for the submarine the *Condor* had reported. He did not spot it and finally decided the report was a false alarm. False sightings happened often in the area. At 4:58 A.M., the net that stretched across the harbor to keep out enemy submarines swung open to let the *Condor* and the *Crossbill* into the harbor.

Because the supply ship *Antares* was coming in from the South Pacific at any moment, the net was left open. When the *Antares* finally reached the harbor, a tug headed out to meet the ship. While the commander of the *Antares* waited for the tug, he spotted a submarine.

He alerted the *Ward*, and this time the *Ward's* commanding officer saw the submarine. It was waiting to follow the *Antares* into the harbor. He gave orders to begin firing. The first shot missed. The second did not. The two-man crew of the Japanese midget submarine became the first casualties at Pearl Harbor, at around 6:45.

The *Ward's* commanding officer reported the sinking to his superiors, but no immediate action was taken. U.S. planes stayed on the ground, and ammunition remained in storage. If action had been taken on the radar sightings and if faster action had been taken after the report of the submarine sinking, Americans would have had about fifty minutes to get their planes in the air. The attack still would have taken place, but U.S. planes would have had a fighting chance.

Code "Tiger"

As Fuchida flew closer to Hawaii, he searched the sky for U.S. planes. He and his men had been flying for an hour and a half when he saw the coast of Hawaii below him. With no U.S. planes in sight, he signaled his men that they had surprised the Americans. At 7:49 his radio operator tapped his keys: *to, to, to,* the first syllable of the Japanese word for "charge." Then the operator tapped *Tora, Tora, Tora.* This was the word for "tiger" and the code to let people on the Japanese carriers know that the U.S. military had been surprised. Fuchida watched as his planes streaked toward Battleship Row.

At 7:55 the planes attacked. They hit the *Raleigh* and the *Utah.* Fuchida's target was the *Nevada,* and his plane headed for it. But the bombardier did not get a good sighting and did not drop his bomb. The plane circled and flew back to the *Nevada.* This time the ship was shrouded with smoke from other burning ships. Fuchida decided not to wait any longer. He gave orders to hit the *Maryland.* For almost thirty-five minutes, men and planes worked together like a well-trained football team.

After the bombers dropped their loads, they met other planes at a prearranged area and flew in groups back to the carriers. Fuchida stayed to take pictures of the damage and to watch the second group of planes carry out its attack. But before the second group arrived, the destroyer *Monaghan* sank another Japanese midget submarine. Fuchida did not see the sinking. Smoke from burning ships and planes hid his view.

They're Saving the *Nevada*

After the first group of Japanese planes left, every American soldier who could move got ready for more planes, which they were sure would come. So when the second group of planes reached Oahu at 8:40 A.M., they were met with gunfire. Guns on the *Tennessee* were fired so fast that the heat stripped the paint off some of them. Within minutes, guns from the *Maryland* and the *Helena* hit three Japanese planes.

Throughout the fighting, fires threatened to engulf almost everybody and everything on the ground. The flaming *Arizona* threatened to set fire to the *Nevada*. Damaged but still afloat, the ship was without its commanding officer. He and several officers had stayed ashore the night before, and they had been trying to get to their ship since the first bomb fell. But Honolulu's roads were clogged with cars filled with other people trying to get to their ships.

When the first torpedoes and bombs fell, Lieutenant Lawrence Ruff was on a nearby ship waiting for church services to begin. He hurried back to the *Nevada* and directed the men above decks while Lieutenant Commander J. F. Thomas directed those below decks. Ensign Taussig continued giving orders from his stretcher. With burning oil lapping at the ship and water flooding below decks, these men made a decision. They would get the *Nevada* out of Battleship Row.

It was an incredible decision. Normally, it took at least two hours to get boilers heated up enough to move a battleship. Tugs had to pull it, nudge it, and ease it out of its berth while the commanding officer navigated. The *Nevada* had neither tugs nor commanding officer, but it had men determined to save their ship. Despite incredible odds, the *Nevada's* boilers were lit, and the ship was cut loose from its mooring. Through smoke that sometimes choked and blinded everyone, and with a hole in its bow as large as a building, the *Nevada* headed for the channel. Cheers erupted from other ships and the survivors who had made it to shore.

As the *Nevada* moved, sailors on its decks tossed ropes

to people in the water and pulled them aboard. Once aboard, they manned the *Nevada's* guns. As the *Nevada* passed the burning *Arizona*, the heat was so intense that the *Nevada's* gunners covered shells with their bodies to keep them from exploding and from killing them and their shipmates.

The Japanese had no intention of letting the *Nevada* escape. The dive bomber that had been heading for the *Helena* changed its course and zeroed in on the *Nevada*. The bomb hit and the ship shook. A second bomb killed the crew at one of the guns and most of the crew at the gun beside it. When a third bomb hit, the ship shuddered— but it kept moving. The *Nevada* became the Japanese bombers' favorite target. If they sank it in the entrance to the channel, the ship would lock up the harbor for months. Despite the hail of ammunition, the *Nevada* moved.

But officers at the 14th Naval District could not take the chance of having the harbor blocked. They raised flags signaling all ships to stay out of the channel. Although Ensign Taussig insisted that the *Nevada* could make it out, Captain Thomas obeyed orders and cut the *Nevada's* engines. It grounded into the mud at Hospital Point at 9:10 A.M. With the ship on fire and taking on water, the *Nevada's* guns kept firing at oncoming planes. Five minutes later, when the commanding officer reached his ship to take command, he saluted the flag raised barely an hour earlier while the band dodged bullets. The flag was torn and dirty, but it was still flying.

The Final Minutes

The Japanese left the seemingly indestructible *Nevada* in the mud and went after destroyers in drydock. Within minutes they had blasted the *Pennsylvania*. Bombs that missed the *Pennsylvania* hit the destroyers *Cassin* and *Downes*. The *Cassin* rolled over onto the *Downes*. At 9:30 the destroyer *Shaw* exploded, showering clothing, mattresses, dishes, furniture, guns, and human limbs in the water and on other ships.

Bombs fell on the *Raleigh*, which was the first ship Fuchida's group hit. The *Raleigh* had stayed afloat, but now the crew struggled to keep it from capsizing. Everything they could break loose or did not need was dumped overboard. Throughout the dumping, gun crews kept firing at the Japanese planes.

At 9:45 Fuchida watched the second group of planes head toward their rendezvous. He took more pictures and then, getting low on gas, headed for the rendezvous area. A couple of planes without directional instruments were circling around. Fuchida led them back to the carriers, to the cheers of everyone aboard.

He found planes ready for a third attack. As soon as planes landed on the carriers, they were refueled, rearmed, and lined up. A third attack had not been planned, and Admiral Chuichi Nagumo, commander in chief of the First Air Fleet, was against it. Still, he asked his officers for their opinions. Many wanted to go back to bomb repair areas so that U.S. ships could not be salvaged, wreck military gas storage tanks so that American planes could not fly, and destroy buildings that supplied electricity.

Although many officers asked to return to the scene of battle, some felt Japan would suffer large numbers of casualties during a third attack. Several officers said their men were exhausted. Some pointed to planes that had staggered back low on gas and peppered with bullet holes. Others said the weather and seas were getting worse and that it would be dangerous to launch planes.

The meeting went on. The point was made that some of the ships in the U.S. Pacific Fleet had been on patrol during the attack. These ships would be searching for the Japanese carriers by now. Some officers suggested that they begin their own search so that they could destroy the ships on patrol. Nagumo listened to everyone's suggestions and arguments and then made the final decision. The Japanese carriers headed home.

3

AMERICA ENTERS THE WAR

By the time Japanese planes left Hawaii, less than two hours after they came, Pearl Harbor was cloaked in fire and smoke. In fear and pain, people begged to die. Some were in shock and did not recognize their best friends standing beside them. At the wounded collection area, pharmacists smashed open medicine lockers to get morphine to ease their patients' pain.

Many people knelt in prayer. One sailor sat at his desk typing over and over again "Now is the time for all good men to come to the aid of their country," while his friends screamed, sobbed, or stared into space around him. Fear paralyzed people, but those who could move, including Hawaii's commanding officers, prepared for a third attack.

Hawaii's Commanding Officers

Lieutenant General Walter C. Short was commander of the Hawaiian Department. His responsibilities included the defense of the U.S. Pacific Fleet while it was in Pearl Harbor and the defense of the Hawaiian Islands. To carry out his responsibilities, General Short had three levels of alerts to help his troops defend the fleet and the islands. Alert 1 was the defense against sabotage and espionage.

The general's fear of sabotage and espionage was the reason U.S. planes were so close together. He believed that planes lined up wing-tip to wing-tip could be guarded with the smallest number of soldiers. On the morning of December 7, Hawaii was on Alert 1.

Alert 2 called for preparing the area against air, land, and submarine attack. Alert 3 called for total defense of Hawaii. Although the army sometimes practiced Alerts 2 and 3, Hawaii usually stayed on Alert 1. Like many military people, General Short believed that the island of Oahu was a fortress and that no one would be crazy enough to attack it. On December 7, Oahu was not put on Alert 3 until 8:40 A.M. By then hundreds of lives had been lost.

Admiral Husband E. Kimmel was commander in chief of the U.S. Pacific Fleet. When the bombing started at 7:55, Admiral Kimmel was at home. One of his officers telephoned to tell him that the *Ward* had sunk an enemy submarine. While they discussed the sinking, a sailor reported to the officer that the Japanese were attacking. When Admiral Kimmel heard the news, he dropped the phone and ran to his backyard. By the time he got outside his ships were burning.

He jumped into his car and reached his office between 8:05 and 8:10. Noise hit him from every direction. It came from dive-bombing planes, exploding torpedoes, aircraft guns, and screams for help. The admiral ordered his planes to take off and destroy enemy planes. But as he watched the attack from his office, he knew his orders could not be carried out.

Like General Short, Admiral Kimmel considered Oahu a fortress. He believed an attack was possible but not probable. He also believed that if the Japanese attacked his ships, they would do it while the ships were at sea, not at Pearl Harbor. To protect his ships at sea, Kimmel had ordered the ships coming into the harbor to turn around before mooring. That way, they could head out faster to help the ships at sea if they were attacked.

Although the two top-ranking officers in Hawaii believed that Japan would not attack Hawaii, one of the officers knew something the other did not know. General Short knew Pearl Harbor was on Alert 1. He had made the decision. And because of the many joint army and navy meetings to discuss defense of the islands, he assumed Admiral Kimmel knew Oahu was on Alert 1. Short's assumption was wrong. Kimmel did not know. He believed that his ships were protected from air, sea, and land attacks twenty-four hours a day. What neither commanding officer knew on the morning of December 7 was that a warning from Washington about a possible attack had been delivered to the island before Japan's planes ever reached Hawaii.

The message was sent by General George C. Marshall, chief of staff of the U.S. Army: "Japanese are presenting at one P.M. eastern standard time today what amounts to an ultimatum. . . . also they were under orders to destroy their code machine immediately. Just what significance the hour set may have we do not know, but be on alert accordingly."

The message reached the RCA office in Honolulu at 7:33 A.M. Because the message was not marked priority, a worker put it with civilian messages to be delivered to Kahili, the area where Short's headquarters were located. The delivery boy put the envelopes for Kahili in his bag and hopped on his bike. He ran into traffic jams caused by people trying to get to their stations and did not reach Fort Shafter until 11:45. After the message was decoded, it went to Short's office. The time was 2:58 P.M. By then General Short and Admiral Kimmel were getting ready for a land invasion of the island that they were already certain would come.

Searching for Friends and Foes

To try to stop a land invasion, U.S. ships at sea and the few planes that could operate searched for Japan's carriers. But with so many U.S. planes destroyed or damaged, the first in the air were unarmed planes that usually carried mail or photographed army and navy drills. Because these planes had no guns, pilots were given rifles as their only protection against armed enemy planes.

Later, better-equipped U.S. planes that had been on patrol when the attack took place and the few that had not suffered much damage took part in the search. But because the officer at Fort Shafter thought the planes on the radar screens at Opana Station were B-17s and had not reported the sightings to his superiors, searchers did not know which direction the enemy planes had come from. And the enemy carriers got away.

While ships and planes searched for the enemy, people looked for friends, and ship officers gave and canceled orders. On the *California*, the captain watched burning oil in the harbor move closer to his ship. At 10:15 he ordered his men to abandon ship. But when the flames cleared the ship, he canceled the order. By the time the cancel order came, many had already jumped overboard. Having made it to safety, only a few obeyed the captain's cancel order.

A crewman still on the ship spotted the American flag lying on the *California's* blood-soaked deck. The flag should have been raised at 8 o'clock, and now, to inspire his shipmates to return, the crewman ran the flag up the pole. When the sailors saw the Stars and Stripes flying over their ship, most went back. They kept the ship from capsizing, but they could not keep it afloat. The scorched *California* settled into the harbor's shallow water.

The *Utah* was in worse shape than the *California*. It lay

in the mud like a beached whale. But rescuers were determined to save the men trapped inside. For hours, they followed the sound of tapping from inside the hull and cut holes to rescue the trapped sailors.

Some men trapped in the overturned *Oklahoma* escaped through portholes that were now under water. One by one, they squeezed through. But a large sailor could not fit through the porthole, and he was left alone to die. Others on the *Oklahoma* were not freed until the next day. One said that being rescued from inside the overturned ship was like being dug out of a grave.

There was no one to save on the *Arizona*. But late in the afternoon, one of its officers, who had been on shore when the attack started, went to see what was left of his ship. He found the ship's flag dragging in the oily water.

Japanese Consul Denies Attack

While planes were still bombing Oahu, the Japanese consul general in Honolulu, Nagao Kita, claimed there was no attack. Even as he read the headline "War! Oahu Bombed by Japanese Planes" on the front page of the *Star-Bulletin*, he did not admit to people questioning him that the Japanese were bombing the island.

When the Hawaiian police arrived at the consulate, they found consulate workers burning papers in a washtub. The police put out the fire and saved some of the secret documents for the FBI and the Navy Department. When one of the officers asked the workers if they knew Pearl Harbor was being attacked, they said they did not know.

It is believed most of them did not know their country was going to attack Hawaii that morning. But it is hard to believe they did not know there was an attack going on. Their office was only a few miles from Pearl Harbor.

Oahu Is Placed under Alert 3

During the early morning, radio stations KGMB and KGU interrupted their regular programs to order military personnel to report to duty and to tell doctors and nurses to report to hospitals. At 11:15 Governor Joseph E. Poindexter read a Proclamation of Emergency over the radio. Then, at 11:42, General Short ordered KGU and KGMB off the air to keep enemy planes from homing in the way Fuchida had earlier in the day.

By afternoon martial law had been proclaimed, and the army took control of the island. Messages that did come over the radio were censored and were short and far between. Under martial law the army controlled the radio, the press, the mail, and telephone and telegraph offices.

People were told to stay off the streets. Blackouts went into effect, and people covered their windows with black paint, shades, or heavy curtains. Block wardens patrolled the streets to make sure no light escaped from windows. Any light, even one as small as a lighted match, could be spotted from the air by enemy planes. People were told to fill their baths with water so that they would have some to drink if the enemy destroyed more water mains. When they heard that the Japanese living on the islands had poisoned the water, panic turned to hysteria. But the poisoned water turned out to be a rumor.

Other rumors spread. The Japanese were landing on Diamond Head. They had captured Waikiki Beach. They had taken the whole north coast. Enemy paratroopers were dropping all over the islands. They were going to attack Wheeler Field and Schofield Barracks again. The Japanese had taken San Francisco and were moving south to Los Angeles.

Some of the rumors racing through Honolulu turned out to be true. The city had been hit by a Japanese bomb and had taken forty hits from Japanese and American guns. Buildings were damaged, four people in a car were blown apart, and a thirteen-year-old girl watching the explosions from her porch was killed.

Janet Yonamine Kishimori, a five-year-old Japanese, was luckier. She was in Sunday school with her brother and sister the morning the bombing started. As the pastor moved the children to a safer building, he told them something terrible had happened at Pearl Harbor. Then he led them in prayer until adults came for them.

When Janet got home, her mother was hiding the picture of Emperor Hirohito, Japan's ruler, which had been on the wall since Janet could remember. But if the picture stayed on the wall now, people would think the family was not loyal to America. For the first time Janet heard the word *war*. When she asked what the word meant, her mother looked so scared that Janet thought monsters must be attacking the world.

Despite the rumors most people in Honolulu went about their business. Jack C. Smith, now an author and syndicated columnist, and his wife, Denise, were on their way home from an all-night party when they saw planes flying over the harbor. Like everyone else on the island, they were used to army and navy drills. When they got home, Smith called his editor at the *Advertiser* to check out the "drill." The editor told him the Japanese were attacking Pearl Harbor. Smith said, "I know." Later he realized that the attack was so unbelievable he had not admitted to anyone that it was happening—not even to himself—until the moment he said the words "I know" to his editor.

Like many others in Hawaii, Smith did not get any sleep that day. He went to the newspaper office to help put out the paper, but the presses were broken, and he spent his time answering the phone. Many calls were from people who wanted to know if the Japanese were really attacking Pearl Harbor. That evening, when Smith went to the roof of the *Advertiser* building to watch the ships still burning in Pearl Harbor, a soldier almost shot him. The soldier thought Smith was a Japanese trying to take over the building and the newspaper.

Now that Oahu was on Alert 3, guards were posted everywhere, and many of them shot at anything that moved. Gunfire set off other guns. When one man pulled the trigger at Kaneohe Air Station, he set off so much firing that people thought the Japanese had launched the third attack everyone said was coming.

The Final Count

While the military guarded against the enemy, doctors and nurses operated around the clock to help the wounded who poured into the hospitals. After their wounds were bandaged, many patients left the hospitals without permission to help others who were wounded. They also helped carry the dead to collection areas. The bodies were ordered to be moved after dark, when few people would be out. And the fewer people who saw the large numbers of dead, the better. Morale was already low, and the sight of all of those bodies would sink morale even lower and make it harder for people to do their jobs.

When the final count was taken, fewer than one hundred Japanese had died. Japan had lost one large submarine, five midget submarines, and twenty-nine planes.

The numbers were much higher for the United States: 2,403 people had died, including civilians, and 1,178 were wounded. Many of the approximately one hundred ships that were in the harbor were sunk or damaged. And almost all of the three hundred planes at the airfields were destroyed or damaged.

The Nation Learns
of the Attack

President Franklin D. Roosevelt learned about the attack fifteen minutes after it started. In Washington the time was 1:40 P.M. EST. He called Secretary of State Cordell Hull to tell him the news. Despite the attack by Japan, Hull kept an appointment with Japanese ambassadors Kichisaburo Nomura and Saburo Kurusu. The meeting was scheduled for 1 P.M., but the ambassadors did not arrive until after 2 o'clock and did not meet with Hull until 2:30. If they had arrived on time, it would have been 7:30 A.M. in Hawaii, twenty-five minutes before the attack began.

Although Hull knew about the attack, he did not mention it to the ambassadors. Angry, he glanced at the papers Nomura gave him. The papers said, among other things, that Japan was breaking diplomatic relations with the United States. When Hull finished reading, he glared at Nomura and said: "In all my fifty years of public service I have never seen a document that was more crowded with infamous falsehoods and distortions—infamous falsehoods and distortions on a scale so huge that I never imagined until today that any Government on this planet was capable of uttering them."

Nomura and Kurusu left without a word. In fact, Nomura only learned of the attack when he got back to his embassy. Later that day, he wrote in his diary: "December 7. The day on which diplomatic relations between Japan and America were severed. . . . The report of our surprise attack against Hawaii reached my ears when I returned home from the state department." Japan's ambassador had not been told his country would attack Pearl Harbor.

Americans learned about the attack in different ways. At the Washington Redskins' last football game of the season twenty-seven thousand people watched the Redskins play the Philadelphia Eagles in Griffith Stadium only a few miles from the White House. Reporters in the press box were the first at the stadium to learn about the bombing. When people close by heard them talking about the attack, the news raced through the crowd. Some people did not believe what they heard. Some did not know where Pearl Harbor was. Almost everyone kept cheering for the Redskins.

Then an announcement came over the loudspeakers paging a general to report to his office. An admiral was also paged. Then more military officers were asked to report to work. A request came for the ambassador from the Philippines to go to his embassy. Despite these announcements, news that the Japanese had attacked Hawaii did not come over the loudspeakers. The manager was afraid that the announcements would panic the crowd.

J. Edgar Hoover, head of the FBI, learned about the bombing while visiting New York. When one of his agents in Honolulu called to tell him of the attack, Hoover did not believe him. To make Hoover believe, the officer held the phone out of his office window so that Hoover could hear the bombs exploding. Then he believed.

President Gives His
War Speech to Congress

General Marshall, Cordell Hull, and advisers to the president went to the White House to discuss the bombing. During their meeting, phone calls came often from Admiral Harold R. Stark, chief of Naval Operations. His information about Pearl Harbor was bleak. Like General Short and Admiral Kimmel in Hawaii, almost everyone in Washington worried that the Japanese would follow the air attacks with a land invasion of Hawaii.

At four o'clock the president learned that Japan had declared war on the United States and the British Empire. Shortly afterward, Roosevelt began dictating the speech he would deliver to Congress the next day, asking that the United States declare war on Japan.

On December 8, at 12:29 P.M., President Roosevelt entered the Capitol to give his speech to Congress and the American people. He opened a black loose-leaf notebook. "Yesterday," the president began, "December 7, 1941, a date which will live in infamy, the United States of America was suddenly and deliberately attacked by naval and air forces of the Empire of Japan. . . . The attack yesterday on the Hawaiian Islands has caused severe damage to the American naval and military forces. . . . Many lives were lost." He talked about the attacks on Malaya, Hong Kong, the Philippines, and the islands of Guam, Wake, and Midway. The speech was over in six minutes. In less than an hour, Congress had declared war on the Japanese Empire.

* * *

The attack on Pearl Harbor affected all Americans. It brought the country closer together. Americans shared with each other their losses and their fears. They also shared the determination to defend their country against Japan. Within days, America added two more nations to its list of enemies. On December 11, Germany and Italy declared war on the United States. The same day, the U.S. Congress declared war on Germany and Italy.

Germany and Italy had already conquered many European countries that were allies of the United States. Although President Roosevelt had sent arms and equipment to help these American allies, by December 1941 most were under enemy occupation. Many Americans, who called themselves isolationists, had demonstrated against the president for sending help. They said that getting involved in European politics was tantamount to dragging the United States into a war. Other Americans supported the president for helping countries in Europe.

These two groups had argued their differences in person and in the press. They were still arguing about it on December 7. Japan ended their arguments. The attack on Pearl Harbor united Americans in one cause. That cause was to defend their freedom.

4

FROM FRIENDS TO ENEMIES

In 1543 while French and Spanish sailors were exploring the North American continent, of which the United States would become a part, Portuguese sailors reached the shores of Japan. These men were the first Europeans the Japanese people had seen. The foreigners were welcomed, and soon other traders stopped at Japan's ports. Missionaries also arrived to try to convert the Japanese people to Christianity.

For years, Japan's rulers tolerated the traders and the missionaries. But as the years passed, Japan's leaders became concerned that the missionaries were converting too many Japanese. They also worried that the Europeans, with their powerful ships and guns, might try to conquer Japan. As a result, foreigners were ordered to leave the country. Only a few Dutch were allowed to stay to run their trading post. This privilege was granted because they had never tried to convert the Japanese. With its ports shut to foreign visitors, Japan began its isolation from the rest of the world. By 1640 the isolation was complete.

This, however, did not stop merchant ships from sailing the Pacific. By the early 1800s more and more captains were asking permission to stop at Japan's ports. The government refused. Some U.S. sailors, however, did enter

Japan. They were shipwrecked, and although the Japanese allowed the sailors into the country, they did not let them leave. Some of the Americans were mistreated and some were killed. Determined to save the sailors, the United States tried to discuss the problem with Japan. Their request was turned down.

Finally, the United States sent ships to Japan to force its rulers to help the captive sailors. The United States also wanted to open trade with Japan. The four ships, sent by President Millard Fillmore and led by Commodore Matthew C. Perry, reached Tokyo Bay on July 8, 1853. On July 14 Perry delivered President Fillmore's letter to the Japanese government and said he would return for an answer.

The Japanese watched the American ships sail from Tokyo Bay. They were painted black, and two of them were run by steam. All four were large and powerful. Japan could not defend itself against those ships. When Perry came back in February 1854, he had with him even more ships. He also was accompanied by two thousand marines and sailors.

The Japanese signed a treaty with the United States on March 31, 1854. The agreement stated that shipwrecked American sailors would be treated well and that U.S. ships could stop at certain Japanese ports to trade and to have repairs made. Soon the Japanese signed treaties with European nations. Japan's two hundred years of isolation were over.

During the years that followed, not everyone in Japan wanted contact with foreigners, and American ships were sometimes fired on. In 1867, Emperor Matsuhito became Japan's leader. Not long after taking power he encouraged his people to learn everything they could from other nations. If Japan was to become a modern nation, it would have to study modern ways.

In time the Japanese began to build industries. They

created stronger military forces through new ideas and technology. They modeled their schools after the American school system. Every year thousands of Japanese students sailed to the United States to study in American schools. Then they returned to Japan and applied their knowledge to helping their country become a stronger and more modern nation.

United States and Japan
Expand in the Pacific

While Japan was changing the way its people lived, the United States was acquiring lands in the west. In 1848, after the United States waged and won a war against Mexico, California became part of the United States. In 1867 the United States bought Alaska. In 1898 it annexed the Republic of Hawaii. The United States also acquired Samoa, the Philippines, Guam, and Wake Island. With its new responsibilities in the Pacific, the United States began to build a larger navy.

For its part, Japan was acquiring more land in the Pacific. In the late 1880s and early 1900s it acquired, among other areas, the southern part of Manchuria, Korea, and Formosa, which is now called Taiwan. During World War I, Japan fought on the same side as the United States, and took control of several Pacific island groups from Germany at the end of the war. The League of Nations made Japan the administrator of those islands. Throughout this time Japan's navy, like the U.S. Navy, continued to grow.

By 1920 Japan had the strongest army and navy in Asia. With territories to protect, the United States felt threatened in the Pacific. The U.S. government invited Japan, Great Britain, and other nations to Washington to discuss a Nine-Power Treaty. The conference began in

November 1921 and ended in February 1922. Each nation represented agreed to respect the others' rights in the Pacific. Each also agreed to limit the size of its navy.

Although Japan signed the treaty, it felt cheated. The rule limit that was worked out allowed Japan to own three major ships for every five major U.S. ships and every five major British ships. With this formula Japan would have a smaller navy than either the United States or Great Britain. But since the United States and Great Britain operated their ships in both the Atlantic and the Pacific, Japan would have supremacy in the Pacific.

Japan also became stronger by colonizing the islands that the League of Nations had permitted it to administer. Through colonization, the Japanese hoped to produce food for its growing population and materials for industrialization. New Japanese colonies would also reduce overcrowding in Japan. By the 1930s thousands of Japanese lived on the island colonies. There they had homes, shrines, businesses, and farms. They also built military bases, which was against the League of Nations agreement.

More Problems with Japan

Japan continued to grow by chipping away at China. In 1931 it invaded northern Manchuria and called the newly conquered land Manchukuo. It also invaded Shanghai and other parts of China. In 1936 Japan withdrew from the naval agreement signed in 1922 and built more major ships to strengthen its navy.

During Japan's invasion of China in 1937 a Japanese plane sank the *Panay*, an American ship, killing a number of Americans. The United States protested with words instead of with guns. Japan answered with an apology and money for the loss of the ship and people. There was a reason for this apology and payment. Japan was still dependent on the United States for oil, iron, tin, nickel, copper, and rubber. Without the materials to build more ships and the oil to keep its military machine working, Japan would have to give up its dream of conquering more land in Asia.

Part of Japan's apology was the promise that Japan would stop its air bombings in China, which were killing thousands of people. When Japan did not end its bombings, however, the United States stopped exporting aircraft and aircraft parts to Japan. In September 1940 Japan invaded French Indochina, which is now Vietnam, and the United States stopped selling all raw materials to Japan except oil.

While Japan was busy in Asia, Adolf Hitler of Germany was busy in Europe. When he invaded Poland on September 1, 1939, England and France declared war on Germany. By 1941 Germany had formed an alliance with Italy and had defeated France, Belgium, the Netherlands, Norway, Denmark, and Luxembourg.

With France and the Netherlands conquered by Germany, and England battling for survival, it was clear to the Japanese the only nation that could stop them from invading the areas that could supply natural resources was the United States. And the strongest weapon the United States had was the Pacific Fleet, based at Pearl Harbor.

Isolationists

Even with its impressive Pacific Fleet stationed at Pearl Harbor, the United States was not ready for war, and President Roosevelt kept asking Congress for billions of dollars for defense. Isolationists, who had worked for years to keep the United States out of war, called him a warmonger. They insisted that continued help to other countries would lead to war. But other Americans cheered

Roosevelt's requests for a stronger defense. They believed that if Hitler conquered Great Britain he would next attack the United States.

Despite protests from isolationists, the United States continued to send planes and ships to Great Britain. The first American ship sunk by German submarines was a merchant marine vessel carrying supplies to Great Britain. After another ship was sunk and one hundred Americans lost their lives, Congress ordered that merchant ships be armed. The isolationists considered this order one more step toward war in Europe and worked even harder to keep the United States out of the fighting. They paid little attention to Japan. Like most Americans, they considered Japan too small and too weak to fight a war with the United States.

The United States and Magic

In 1940 Japan also did not consider itself ready for war with the United States. So it kept diplomatic talks open in Washington and hoped for a peaceful solution to its problems. But it prepared for war.

The United States knew Japan was preparing for war. In August 1940, after almost two years of work, the U.S. Army Signal Intelligence Service (SIS) had broken Japan's diplomatic codes. The hardest diplomatic code to break was the one called Purple. The breaking of Purple and other Japanese diplomatic codes became known as Magic. With Magic, the U.S. government listened to everything sent from Japan's Foreign Office to its embassies around the world. Many of these messages hinted that Japan was preparing to attack the United States.

Magic was so secret that few people in the U.S. government and military knew it existed. Its messages were carried in locked pouches to the White House, the State

Department, and several other government and military officials. The information was read and then returned to SIS.

Even President Roosevelt could not keep copies of these messages in his files. Secrecy was vital. If Japan learned that the United States had broken its diplomatic codes, it would change them, and the United States could no longer monitor Japan's actions.

But because of Magic the United States *did* know what Japan was doing. If Japan conquered more of China or tried to invade the islands belonging to Great Britain, France, and the Netherlands, the United States would not stand by and let it happen. In addition to helping its allies, the United States was also responsible for protecting the Philippines and its important military bases there.

The U.S. military bases on Guam and Wake and Midway islands also had to be protected. U.S. ships had refueled at Guam for years. Wake not only served the U.S. military, it also refueled civilian planes on their way across the Pacific. And Midway was the last defense between Japan and Hawaii. All of these places were close to Japan's military bases. Guam was less than 100 miles (160 km) from Saipan, and Wake was near Kwajalein in the Marshall Islands. Despite all of this, Hawaii's commanding officers, Admiral Kimmel and General Short, did not receive Magic's messages because their names were not on the U.S. intelligence list of people cleared to receive them.

Magic also helped the U.S. government learn what was going on between Japan and Germany. On September 27, 1940, Japan signed the Tripartite Pact with Germany and its ally Italy. The three countries agreed to help each other with political, economic, and military needs. Although Germany and Italy were too busy fighting their war in Europe to give much help to Japan in the Pacific, the

United States considered the treaty a move toward war by Japan.

U.S. ambassador to Japan Joseph C. Grew worried so much about the breakdown of relations between the United States and Japan that on December 14, 1940, he wrote to President Roosevelt: "It seems to me increasingly clear that we are bound to have a showdown some day, and the principal question at issue is whether it is to our advantage to have that showdown sooner or have it later."

Some people in the U.S. government felt that Grew was right. A showdown with Japan was inevitable. Many believed the showdown would occur somewhere in the West and South Pacific so that Japan could get the raw materials it needed. Some thought a showdown would be closer to Hawaii.

Hardly anyone thought Pearl Harbor would be Japan's target. It would not be foolish enough to attack a fortress. Six to eight battleships were usually stationed there. There were also aircraft carriers, destroyers, cruisers, submarines, minesweepers, and miscellaneous boats. The U.S. Navy also had planes to defend Pearl Harbor from the sky. The Army Air Corps had bombers at Hickam Field. Fighter planes crowded Wheeler Field. The army trained with modern equipment and had guns aimed toward the sea, ready to stop enemy ships from attacking the shore.

The harbor was too shallow for enemy planes to carry out a successful attack from the sky. The best chance anyone would have of damaging U.S. ships would be with submarines. But that danger had been eliminated by putting a net across the entrance to the harbor.

Despite these obstacles, Japan prepared to attack Pearl Harbor.

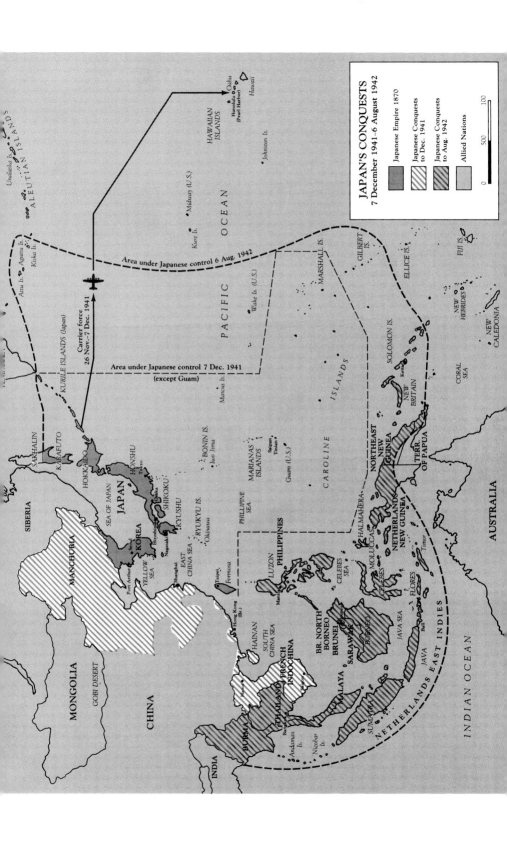

JAPAN'S CONQUESTS
7 December 1941–6 August 1942

Japanese Empire 1870

Japanese Conquests
to Dec. 1941

Japanese Conquests
to Aug. 1942

Allied Nations

0   500   100

ALEUTIAN ISLANDS

Unalaska Is.

Attu Is.   Agattu Is.
Kiska Is.

Area under Japanese control 6 Aug. 1942

Oahu
Honolulu
(Pearl Harbor)

Hawaii

HAWAIIAN
ISLANDS

Johnston Is.

Midway (U.S.)

Kure Is.

PACIFIC   OCEAN

KURILE ISLANDS (Japan)

Carrier force
26 Nov.–7 Dec. 1941

Area under Japanese control 7 Dec. 1941
(except Guam)

Wake Is. (U.S.)

MARSHALL IS.

GILBERT
IS.

ELLICE IS.

FIJI IS.

SAKHALIN

KARAFUTO

HOKKAIDO

HONSHU

SEA OF JAPAN

JAPAN

KOREA

Seoul

KYUSHU

SHIKOKU

RYUKYU IS.

Okinawa

Marcus Is.

BONIN IS.
Iwo Jima

MARIANAS
ISLANDS

Saipan
Tinian

Guam (U.S.)

CAROLINE   ISLANDS

SOLOMON IS.

NEW
BRITAIN

Rabaul

NORTHEAST
NEW
GUINEA

TERR.
OF PAPUA

CORAL
SEA

NEW
HEBRIDES

NEW
CALEDONIA

SIBERIA

MANCHURIA

Port Arthur

YELLOW
SEA

Shanghai

EAST
CHINA SEA

Taipei

Formosa

PHILIPPINE
SEA

LUZON

PHILIPPINES

Manila

HALMAHERA

MOLUCCAS

CELEBES
SEA

NETHERLANDS
NEW GUINEA

Timor

MONGOLIA

GOBI DESERT

CHINA

HONG KONG
(Br.)

HAINAN

SOUTH
CHINA SEA

BR. NORTH
BORNEO
BRUNEI

SARAWAK

BORNEO

CELEBES

FLORES

JAVA SEA

Bali

INDIA

BURMA

THAILAND

FRENCH
INDOCHINA

Hanoi

MALAYA

Bangkok

Singapore

Andaman
Is.

Nicobar
Is.

SUMATRA

NETHERLANDS   EAST   INDIES

JAVA

AUSTRALIA

INDIAN   OCEAN

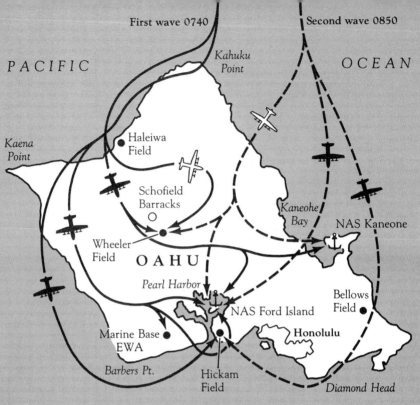

First wave 0740   Second wave 0850

PACIFIC   OCEAN

Kahuku Point

Kaena Point

Haleiwa Field

Schofield Barracks

Kaneohe Bay

NAS Kaneone

Wheeler Field

OAHU

Pearl Harbor

Bellows Field

Marine Base EWA

NAS Ford Island

Honolulu

Barbers Pt.

Hickam Field

Diamond Head

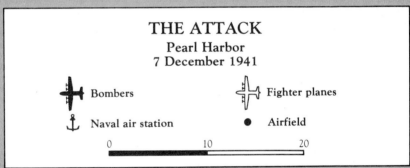

THE ATTACK
Pearl Harbor
7 December 1941

Bombers   Fighter planes

Naval air station   ● Airfield

0   10   20

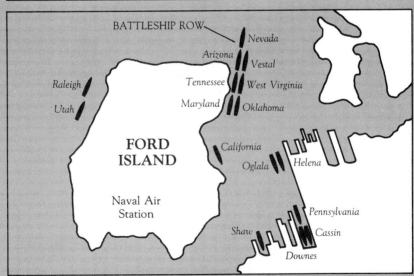

BATTLESHIP ROW

Nevada

Arizona   Vestal

Tennessee   West Virginia

Raleigh   Maryland   Oklahoma

Utah

California

FORD ISLAND   Oglala   Helena

Naval Air Station

Pennsylvania

Shaw   Cassin

Downes

These two aerial photographs were taken during the
sneak attack of December 7, 1941. (Top) A
Japanese plane circles the air near the site of
what is believed to be where the first bomb was
dropped on Pearl Harbor. (Bottom) Japanese torpedoes
leave tracks of bright white streaks in the water
as they head for their targets on Battleship Row.

The USS Shaw (top) explodes while, below,
American sailors fight the flames that engulfed their
battleship, the USS West Virginia. Note the U.S.
flag still flying against the smoke-blackened sky.

*A jumbled mass of wreckage (foreground) is
all that remained of two U.S. Navy destroyers,
the* Downes *(left) and the* Cassin.

(Above) Barracks and hangar facilities on Hickam Field were not spared from aerial Japanese bombing. (Right) The wreckage of the USS Arizona.

Facing page: (Top) The huge battleship, the USS Utah, capsized in Pearl Harbor after it was bombed by the Japanese. (Bottom) A Japanese sentry stands guard on the deck of the 15,000-ton U.S. ship President Harrison. The vessel was the largest Allied ship captured on the day Pearl Harbor was raided.

On December 8, banner headlines announced to the nation what happened in Pearl Harbor. That day President Roosevelt (below) appeared before Congress and asked for an immediate declaration of war on Japan.

Emperor Hirohito of Japan was considered a god-king by many of his people. Although he may have resisted Japan's entry into World War II, he was apparently powerless to restrain the Japanese military. Nonetheless he was instrumental in influencing Japan to surrender to the Allies in 1945.

Vice-Admiral Chuichi Nagumo
Commander of
Operation Hawaii

Minoru Genda
Lt. Commander of
the Imperial Japanese Navy

Hideki Tojo
Japanese premier
(1941–1944)

Admiral Isoroku Yamamoto (left), shown here with Admiral M. Osumi, was commander in chief of Japan's Imperial Navy. (Below) This chart of Pearl Harbor was reportedly found in a captured Japanese submarine. Japanese symbols drawn on the map indicate the anchorage of U.S. ships and details of military establishments around the inner harbor of Pearl Harbor.

Lt. Commander Mitsuo Fuchido, flight leader of the Pearl Harbor attack

Gen. George C. Marshall (left), chief of staff of the U.S. Army, confers with Secretary of War Henry L. Stimson a month following the Pearl Harbor attack.

Frank Knox
U.S. Secretary of the Navy
(1940–1944)

Joseph C. Grew
U.S. Ambassador to Japan
(1932–1941)

(Above) Rear Admiral Patrick N. L. Bellinger
(left) and Maj. Gen. Frederick L. Martin had
cautioned in a report that a surprise raid on
Pearl Harbor could cripple the U.S. Pacific Fleet.

Several investigations, like the one (far top) conducted by the Senate committee in November 1945, attributed the success of the Japanese attack to the errors in judgment of Admiral Husband E. Kimmel (above) and Maj. Gen. Walter C. Short (right). The two officers were relieved of their respective duties as commander in chief of the U.S. Pacific Fleet and commander of the Hawaiian department.

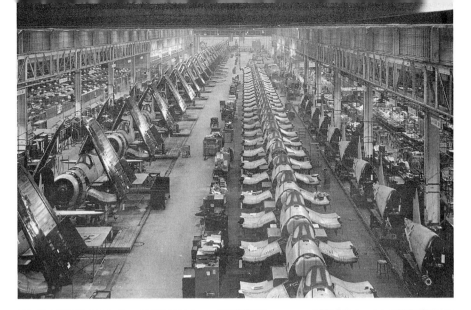

*America prepares for war: (top) This airplane
factory in Stratford, Connecticut, produced over six
thousand Corsair fighter planes used in World War
II. (Bottom) Defense workers wave flags during
the dedication of a Philadelphia armor-plate plant.*

Anti-Japanese sentiment ran high in the country after the Pearl Harbor raid, but many Japanese Americans actually served in the U.S. military during the Second World War.

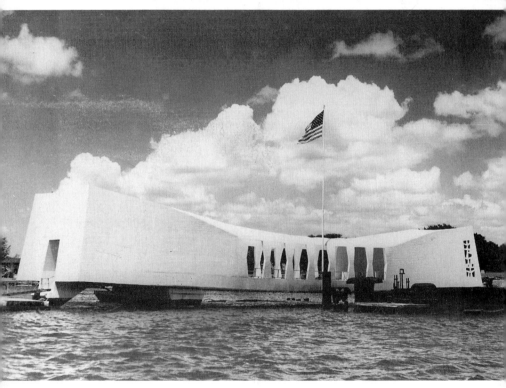

The USS Arizona Memorial was built atop the sunken hull of the ill-fated battleship that is also the grave of about 1,000 crewmen who died on December 7, 1941.

5

TEAM PLAYERS

Although Japan prepared for war, most people in that country did not want war with the United States. And the United States did not want war with Japan. So the two countries tried to solve their problems through diplomacy. But even the ambassadors from the United States and Japan doubted that diplomacy would succeed.

On January 1, 1941, Ambassador Grew wrote in his diary "With all our desire to keep America out of war and at peace with all nations, especially Japan, it would be the height of folly to allow ourselves to be lulled into a feeling of false security. . . . Japan, not we, is on the warpath."

Ambassador Kichisaburo Nomura

Ambassador Kichisaburo Nomura met with Grew on January 20, three days before Nomura sailed for the United States as Japan's ambassador. When the job was first offered to Nomura in the fall of 1940, he refused. He had retired from the Japanese navy as an admiral, and he was enjoying his retirement.

Nomura's government finally convinced him that it was his duty to become ambassador to the United States, but he warned his superiors not to expect miracles. Relations between the two countries were so strained that he might not succeed in bringing them closer together. When he sailed from Japan on January 23, 1941, he still felt there was little he could do to ease the tensions between Japan and the United States.

Nomura presented his credentials to President Roosevelt on February 14, 1941. The president met Nomura as a friend and said he would call him Admiral. This was what the president had called Nomura years earlier when he worked in Washington. At the time, President Roosevelt had been an assistant secretary of the navy. The title of admiral pleased Nomura, and the president's friendliness gave him hope that maybe differences between their countries could be resolved on the diplomatic level.

Isoroku Yamamoto

Admiral Isoroku Yamamoto also worried about war with the United States. As commander in chief of Japan's navy he felt it was his duty to conquer areas in the Pacific that were rich with natural resources, especially oil. Without oil his modern ships and well-trained sailors would be useless. But Yamamoto also believed that if he attacked anywhere in the West and South Pacific, the U.S. Pacific Fleet based at Pearl Harbor would come after him and his ships.

Yamamoto was not afraid of a fight, but he knew the power of U.S. ships. As a student at Harvard twenty years earlier and later while working in Washington, he had been impressed by the wealth and technology of the United States, which led him to believe that the U.S. military was the strongest in the world. Despite this strength, Yamamoto told Japan's premier, he would fight the United States to the death. He also warned the premier that the U.S. military was so powerful it would eventually defeat Japan, and Japan would lose face around the world.

Yamamoto respected Nomura, and his appointment as ambassador pleased him. But like Nomura, Yamamoto doubted that problems between Japan and the United States could be solved through diplomatic negotiations. Although he hoped for peace, he planned for war.

At the end of 1940 Yamamoto started talking carefully but seriously to some of his officers about a possible attack on Pearl Harbor. They discussed Japan's surprise attack in 1905 on Russian ships during the Russo-Japanese War. The attack had been carried out with such surprise that the Russian fleet was caught in the harbor like sitting ducks. If Japan had surprised Russia at Port Arthur without planes, it should be able to surprise the United States at Pearl Harbor with planes.

By destroying the U.S. Pacific Fleet, Yamamoto could conquer the West and South Pacific without interference from the United States. The idea was so incredible that the discussions Yamamoto had with his officers usually ended with the word "impossible." But the admiral could not shake the idea. By January 1941 he shared his "impossible" plan with other officers.

When more than one person knows something, it's hard to keep the information secret. In January a rumor started in Japan about a possible attack on Pearl Harbor. Peru's minister to Japan heard the rumor and told the secretary of the U.S. embassy. The secretary told Ambassador Grew. Grew did not quite believe the rumor, but he had known the Peruvian minister for a long time and he trusted him. On January 27 Grew sent a coded message by telegram to the U.S. State Department and another to the Navy Department.

Naval Intelligence in Washington sent the message to the Far Eastern Office of Naval Intelligence (ONI) in

Hawaii, but Grew's message did not worry the chief of ONI. There had been talk about a Japanese attack on Pearl Harbor for years; in fact, the idea had become a joke in Japan. Also, for years Japanese authors had written stories about fictional assaults on Pearl Harbor. But the chief investigated the rumor anyway and then reported that Japan's army and navy had no plans to attack Pearl Harbor.

Husband E. Kimmel

Admiral Husband E. Kimmel became commander in chief of the U.S. Pacific Fleet (CinCPAC) on February 1, 1941. Born in Henderson, Kentucky, on February 26, 1882, he had graduated from the U.S. Naval Academy in 1904, the same year Admiral Yamamoto graduated from Japan's naval academy.

Each rose to his position as commander with personal navy files bulging with praise from his superiors. As they rose in rank, each learned how to pick the best people for his staff and encouraged those people to speak up if they were in disagreement. But each had a temper that some-times kept those people silent. Despite this, each had the loyalty of his staff and crew. In 1941 there was no hint that the attack on Pearl Harbor would have a profound effect on both their careers.

Even before Kimmel took command of CinCPAC, he knew the importance of Pearl Harbor to the United States. It was the only place within thousands of miles where the Pacific Fleet could be repaired and restocked. Within days of taking over as commander in chief, Kimmel wrote to Admiral Harold R. Stark, chief of Naval Operations.

Kimmel asked for more people, ships, and equipment to make his fleet safer and stronger. He was told that the navy would do whatever it could to help but he must keep in mind that with the war in Europe, U.S. ships and equipment were needed more in the Atlantic than in the Pacific.

The war between Great Britain and Germany was going badly for Great Britain, and German submarines sank British ships with alarming regularity. In April, to help Great Britain and to be better prepared for war with Germany, the U.S. Atlantic Fleet was reorganized. Because of the reorganization Stark warned Kimmel that some of his ships might be moved from the Pacific to the Atlantic. Stark kept Kimmel's temper in check by telling him that the people in the Navy Department were still discussing what to do. Disappointed that he did not get the additional ships he wanted and worried that he might lose some of his ships he already had, Kimmel continued writing letters.

Although he believed Pearl Harbor was a fortress, as commander in chief Kimmel also had to be prepared for anything that would affect his ships and their crews. He became curious about how enemies would attack Pearl Harbor if they were foolish enough to try. To get answers about attack possibilities, he asked one of his officers, Rear Admiral Patrick N. L. Bellinger, to write a report in collaboration with Major General Frederick L. Martin, the Army Air Corps Commander in the Hawaiian Islands.

After studying the problem, Bellinger and Martin reported that a surprise raid on Pearl Harbor could cripple the Pacific Fleet so badly that the United States might not be able to strike back at the enemy for months. They warned that submarines would take part in the attack. And they said that the most dangerous kind of attack would come from planes launched from carriers within 300 miles (480 km) of Hawaii. What Martin and Bellinger did not know was that they were predicting what Yamamoto was planning at the very time they were writing their report.

As accurate as the report was, Martin and Bellinger

had written it with the belief that a declaration of war would come before an attack. A declaration of war was the code of honor among nations, and most people in the U.S. government and the military believed that an enemy would not attack without declaring its intentions. This declaration would give the Pacific Fleet and the Hawaiian Department time to prepare.

Kimmel and his superiors in Washington thought the Martin–Bellinger report provided good defensive information, and they agreed with what the two officers had written. But there was a problem. The report also suggested that the U.S. Navy and Army run daily patrols in and over the waters around Hawaii to search for enemy ships and planes. Unfortunately, there were not enough people and equipment in Hawaii for daily patrols. Kimmel wrote more letters to Washington, asking for more people and equipment. Instead of getting some, he lost some.

The Navy Department had decided, after weeks of discussion, that there was not enough naval power in the Atlantic to protect ships owned by Great Britain. The Atlantic Fleet also had to defend the eastern coast of the United States and the Panama Canal, a major route from the Atlantic to the Pacific. After more discussions, the Navy Department decided that taking ships from Pearl Harbor to protect the Atlantic would not put the Pacific in jeopardy. Over his protests, Kimmel lost one-fourth of his fleet to the Atlantic.

Walter C. Short

Lieutenant General Walter C. Short arrived in Hawaii on February 7, 1941, to take over as commander of the Hawaiian Department. Born in Fillmore, Illinois, on March 30, 1880, he had graduated from the University of Illinois in 1902 and become an army officer that year.

Short's job in Hawaii was to protect the islands and the Pacific Fleet, while in port, from enemy attack.

Like Kimmel, Short wrote letters to Washington. He told his superiors that he needed more people, more military supplies, and more planes. His letters went to General George C. Marshall, chief of staff of the U.S. Army. Like Kimmel, Short did not get what he asked for. But unlike Kimmel, he did not lose people and equipment.

In one of his letters Short asked for more radar equipment to spot planes coming toward the islands. And he asked for pursuit planes. (Pursuit planes are what we now call fighter planes.) Again, Short did not get the radar or the pursuit planes. Whatever equipment the United States could spare was used to help England.

Japan Organizes Its First Air Fleet

While Kimmel and Short tried to get people and equipment, Yamamoto was receiving what he needed to carry out Operation Hawaii. During a war, as commander in chief of the Combined Fleet, Yamamoto had the authority to plan attacks, and he and several carefully picked officers developed their plans.

But Yamamoto did not want to wait for war. He believed an air attack on Pearl Harbor, not a declaration of war, should begin hostilities. Knowing the strength of the U.S. military, he also believed that if the attack was not a total surprise, hundreds of Japanese lives and much equipment would be lost.

In April, while the United States was reorganizing the Atlantic Fleet, Japan organized a task force, called the First Air Fleet, built around a concentration of aircraft carriers. The Japanese had talked about such a reorganization since early 1940, and Yamamoto was lucky that the fleet was formed in time for Operation Hawaii. Now Japan's aircraft carriers could transport hundreds of planes within striking distance of their targets. This was something Yamamoto wanted and needed.

But when Admiral Chuichi Nagumo was given command of the First Air Fleet, Yamamoto thought his luck had gone from good to bad. Nagumo was an excellent officer, but he had little training or interest in fighting a war with planes. From the day he heard about Yamamoto's plan Nagumo had said it would not work. He told Yamamoto it would be too difficult for so many ships to sail so far without being seen by U.S. ships or planes. And refueling ships in the middle of the ocean would be too dangerous, especially if the sea was rough.

And what about the weather? No one could plan the weather. Statistics showed that in the northern Pacific usually only seven days in a month were safe enough to refuel ships. If ships could not be refueled, Operation Hawaii would fail.

Minoru Genda

Commander Minoru Genda was one of the most brilliant young officers in the Japanese Navy. At the beginning of October 1940 he was assigned to the First Naval Air Wing. The idea of using planes as a defense strategy was new, and Genda began to think about the best way to employ them during combat. Then he saw a newsreel in a Tokyo theater that showed four American carriers moving in a single line.

Japanese carriers usually sailed in twos, and Genda had been wondering about the best way to get planes from one pair of carriers to meet with planes from other carriers and form a large attack group. After he saw the newsreel, he ordered the carriers to sail together in a larger group. This allowed their planes to gather quickly and to head for their targets in formation.

In February 1941 Genda was assigned to Yamamoto's Operation Hawaii. His comment was that the plan was difficult but not impossible; however, he turned down some of Yamamoto's ideas. One was that planes and their crews would not be recovered after they left their carriers and carried out their attacks. Another was that planes would take off from carriers about 500 miles (800 km) from Hawaii. From that distance they would not have enough gas to return to their carriers. After they dropped their bombs, the planes would fly toward the carriers until their gas ran out. Then the pilots would ditch in the Pacific, where submarines might be able to pick them up. Genda told Yamamoto these were plans for suicide missions, and they were scrapped.

For several years Genda had stressed that the best way to attack an enemy was with planes from carriers and with submarines. He believed in his plan so strongly that he wrote a report saying battleships were becoming useless for war. Whether Genda was right or wrong, he was the person Yamamoto needed for Operation Hawaii.

Genda soon came up with a plan for Yamamoto. The attack should be made around dawn and must be a total surprise. Carriers would have to refuel at sea. Bombers should concentrate on U.S. ships and planes, and the attack should include torpedo, dive, and high-level bombing.

Genda also believed the air attack should be followed by a land attack. With the Pacific Fleet crippled and Hawaii occupied, the U.S. military would be pushed back to the west coast of the United States. Japan would control the Pacific and the war. But the land attack plan was turned down. For the rest of his life Genda believed his strategy would have been the best plan for Japan.

During the months of planning, Genda was not without doubts that Operation Hawaii would succeed. Hawaii was thousands of miles from Japan. The United States had a powerful fleet in the Pacific. Pearl Harbor was too shallow for torpedo bombing. There were airfields filled with planes all over the area: Wheeler, Hickam, Ewa, Kaneoke. Within minutes those planes could be in the air to defend the harbor and all of Hawaii. Despite these obstacles Genda never stopped working on and improving Yamamoto's plans. Without his work and improvements Japan's Operation Hawaii might not have succeeded.

6

SPIES, SPIES, SPIES

Shortly after President Roosevelt sent the Pacific Fleet to Hawaii in May 1940, the Japanese consul general in Hawaii, Kiichi Gunji, received a message from Japan. He was to collect information about ships in Pearl Harbor and send it to Japan's Foreign Office.

Japan used two kinds of espionage in foreign countries. One was run by consulates and was called legal espionage. The other was run by trained spies and was called illegal espionage. Legal espionage included getting information from conversations or newspapers and by watching military equipment and movement in unrestricted areas. Illegal espionage included buying secret information from informants or going into restricted areas to gather material that the spies could not get any other way. It is believed that Japan did not use illegal spying in Hawaii during the 1940s.

When Gunji told his assistant, Otojiro Okuda, to gather the information requested, put it in code, and send it by commercial telegraph to Japan, Okuda protested. He said spying was not a consular officer's duty. Besides, it was dangerous. Gunji assured Okuda that he would not be in any danger. All he had to do was read the newspapers and report what he read about the U.S. military. Okuda finally agreed to take part in legal spying.

When Gunji was transferred back to Japan on September 11, 1940, Okuda became acting consul general until Gunji's replacement arrived. With new responsibilities, Okuda did not have time to read the newspapers as thoroughly as he had done before. Also, he found fewer and fewer stories about ship and plane movement. Although the U.S. government was not censoring the newspapers, it had decided to keep certain information about military movements secret. That secret information was what Okuda needed.

Okuda decided to find an agent who could get what the Foreign Office wanted. He thought about hiring someone of Japanese descent who was living in Hawaii. But whom could he trust? Finally, he chose the consulate's treasurer, Kohichi Seki, as his agent. Seki trained to become a spy by learning to identify pictures of ships in a reference book, *Jane's Fighting Ships*. After two months, he began spying on U.S. ships in Pearl Harbor.

Seki did not need spying experience to do his work. He usually took a taxi from the consulate to Pearl Harbor, only 7 miles (11 km) away, to see which ships were in port and which ones were out to sea. Then he wrote what he saw and gave the papers to Okuda. After reading them, Okuda had them coded and sent to Japan by telegraph.

Although taxi drivers usually do not pay attention to where they take their customers, Seki thought it would be safer and more practical if he had a regular driver. Richard Masayuki Kotoshirodo, a worker at the consulate, was hired to drive Seki around. Kotoshirodo was a native of Hawaii and knew the island well. Seki used that knowledge to do his work.

By the end of February, Seki was able to tell Okuda and the Foreign Office that part of the U.S. fleet was away from port for a week and part was in port for a week. Then the ships that were at sea changed places with the ships in the harbor. The fleet's routine was exactly what Yamamoto needed to plan Operation Hawaii.

On March 14, 1941, Japan's consul general, Nagao Kita, arrived in Hawaii to take charge of the Japanese consulate. He had been instructed to continue the legal spying on U.S. military installations. To help him do his job, Takeo Yoshikawa arrived on March 27. On the ship that brought him to Hawaii, Yoshikawa used the alias Tadashi Morimura. He was known by that name to everyone at the consulate except Okuda and Kita. Yoshikawa was given the title of chancellor in the consulate, and his co-workers were told he was a junior diplomat. But Yoshikawa, alias Morimura, was a trained spy.

Yoshikawa's taxi driver on his sight-seeing tours was John Yoshige Mikami. Mikami's hobby was studying the U.S. Navy's business, and he liked to share what he knew with anyone who would listen. Yoshikawa listened. And he observed. Whenever they got near a military installation, Yoshikawa asked Mikami questions any tourist would ask. By doing this he could get the information he needed and not arouse suspicion. But Yoshikawa quickly learned that he could trust Mikami, and they worked together often. Taxi driver Kotoshirodo, who had worked with Seki, also worked with Yoshikawa.

Yoshikawa soon had several spying locations. One of his favorites was the pier at Pearl City. From there he could see Pearl Harbor and the naval air strips on Ford Island. He could not go to the pier every day because he did not want anyone to become suspicious. So he went two or three times a week, wearing different clothes each time.

In his messages to the Foreign Office, Yoshikawa always reported the ships in Pearl Harbor by name. In May, after some of Kimmel's ships were sent to the Atlantic to help convoy ships for Great Britain, the names of the battleships *Idaho*, *Mississippi*, and *New Mexico* were not on his list. Later in the month three cruisers were missing from the list. Yamamoto and Genda planned their attack from these detailed reports.

Yoshikawa used his tourist cover often and usually dressed in bright Hawaiian shirts. As a tourist, he bought postcards with pictures of Battleship Row and other U.S. military areas and studied them for his reports to Japan. Also, because tourists seldom traveled alone, he took girls on sight-seeing plane rides over Oahu.

From the air Yoshikawa could see the airfields, and he made mental notes of how many runways the fields had and which directions they ran. He counted the hangars so that he could report the approximate number of planes at each field. Tourist planes were not allowed over Pearl Harbor because air space in the area was restricted. But Yoshikawa could see the harbor in the distance and confirm that the information he had gathered was accurate.

On one of his sight-seeing trips in Mikami's taxi, Yoshikawa tried to go into the Schofield Barracks area. The guard stopped them, not because Yoshikawa was a spy but because the taxi did not have the right plates to get on the base. A Japanese spy, dressed in a bright shirt, could enter a military base, but a car without the proper plates could not.

Yoshikawa gathered enough information to draw military maps of Oahu and other islands and to make detailed notes about ship movements. One of his notes was that there were many ships in port on Saturdays and Sundays, and thousands of officers and enlisted men were on leave during the weekends. He also made extensive notes of the comings and goings of American planes; he could report when planes took off from Wheeler and Hickam fields and when they came back.

In Japan, Yamamoto and his officers read every map and every note Yoshikawa sent. Despite all of his work,

Yoshikawa was never told that Japan was planning to attack Pearl Harbor. But after several months of receiving messages from Japan that requested more and more information, he suspected that an attack would come.

U.S. Intelligence and Magic

While Yoshikawa was getting his information on U.S. military installations in Hawaii, SIS continued reading Japanese secret diplomatic messages with Magic. Because of Magic, SIS knew the consulate in Honolulu was gathering information about the Pacific Fleet and sending it to Japan. In spite of this the consulate was not closed. If the United States ordered the consulate closed, Japan would know its codes had been broken, and they would be changed. It could take months, maybe years, for SIS to break new codes. So the Foreign Office and Yamamoto continued to receive the information Yoshikawa gathered during his "tourist" trips around Hawaii.

Wonderful as Magic was, it was not perfect. There were so many messages sent from Japan to its consulates it would have been difficult to keep up with them had they been in English. But the messages were coded and in Japanese. Coded messages from Germany also had to be decoded. They piled up in the U.S. intelligence offices for lack of people to decode and translate. Also, there were not enough radio lines to send all of the information, so the messages were usually sent to Washington by air mail. If the weather was bad, they went by train or ship. Often, by the time the messages were read, it was too late to do anything with the information in them.

But secrets are discovered in strange ways. The secret that the United States was reading Japan's messages to its consulates was discovered by German agents. Word of this reached the Japanese ambassador in Berlin, and he told

Foreign Minister Yosuke Matsuoka, who was in Germany at the time. Matsuoka informed the Foreign Office in Japan, and it sent the information to Ambassador Nomura. When the people at SIS translated this message, they thought it was the end of Magic. Now that the Japanese knew the United States was reading their consulate messages, they would change the codes. But Japan apparently did not believe SIS could break its codes and did not change them.

Magic, however, did not tell SIS everything it wanted to know. Japan's Foreign Office seldom sent military information to its diplomats. So SIS received little information about Japan's navy and army through Magic. And Japan's military codes were so hard to break, SIS could read only about 10 percent of what it picked up.

Spy Watchers

Many people in the U.S. government could have used Magic. But, like Admiral Kimmel and General Short, they were not on the list of people cleared to receive Magic's messages. Among those not on the list were Robert L. Shivers, head of the Federal Bureau of Investigation (FBI) in Hawaii; Captain Irving Mayfield, head of the Hawaiian Naval District Intelligence Office (DIO); and Lieutenant Colonel George W. Bicknell, chief investigative officer for the Hawaiian Department. If they had been on Magic's list, they could have saved themselves a lot of time and work.

Shivers was in charge of espionage cases that involved civilians who did not work for the U.S. Navy or Army. Mayfield investigated espionage involving navy personnel, including people who were not in the service but who worked for the navy. Bicknell investigated espionage involving army personnel and civilians who worked for the army. These three men met once a week to discuss espionage activity on the islands.

Shivers was so sure that people working in the Japanese consulate were spying that he asked J. Edgar Hoover, head of the FBI, for more people to help him investigate workers there. Shivers did not get them, and his staff was too small to give much time to possible spying in the consulate.

Mayfield did not believe employees in the consulate were actually spying, but he thought they might be working for agents who were doing illegal spying. Mayfield was so convinced of this that he tried to get copies of Japan's cablegrams from the telegraph companies in Hawaii. But releasing cablegrams from their files was illegal, and the companies refused. Desperate for information from the consulate, Mayfield wiretapped the phone lines. However, consulate employees did not talk about classified information over the phone, so the taps did not uncover any spies.

Even if spy activity had been found in the Honolulu consulate, little could have been done. Yoshikawa, Seki, and Kita had not done anything illegal. As consuls they could move around the island legally as long as they did not conduct illegal spying.

So Yamamoto continued to gather information about the U.S. military in Hawaii, and U.S. intelligence continued its counterespionage with Magic.

PERSISTENCE IS POWER

During a meeting at Emperor Hirohito's palace on September 6, 1941, much of the talk was about war against the United States. The emperor was not pleased with the warlike talk from his military officers. After much discussion they agreed that diplomatic negotiations should continue and every effort should be made to reach a peaceful agreement. But it was also decided that there should be an October 15 deadline on the negotiations. After that date, Japan should be ready for war with the United States.

On September 12, the yearly war games (make-believe battles fought on paper) began in Tokyo. Plans for control of the Philippines, Malaya, the Dutch East Indies, and other areas of the West and South Pacific were top priority in the minds of most of the admirals and staff officers who took part. They called the plans the Southern Operation.

But Yamamoto also had Operation Hawaii on his mind. When rehearsals for the Southern Operation ended, he shared his Operation Hawaii plans with about thirty carefully chosen officers. He invited them into what he called his secret room and received their promise not to discuss what was said there with anyone else.

When the war games ended on September 17, the officers sworn to secrecy agreed that Operation Hawaii seemed possible on paper. But Admiral Nagumo, who was responsible for carrying out Yamamoto's plans, was still worried.

How could he sneak his ships across the Pacific without being seen by U.S. planes and submarines? What if the U.S. Navy learned about the attack and met his task force with a surprise of its own? And what about refueling his carriers in the rough seas of the Northern Pacific?

War games were one thing, Nagumo said, but war with real enemies and real ships was something different. Like Yamamoto, Nagumo was ready to die for his country. But if he had to go to his death, he wanted to go fighting with the odds on his side. Yamamoto promised he would do everything he could to give Nagumo the best odds during Operation Hawaii.

Aerial Torpedo Bombing

When Operation Hawaii had been discussed in January, one of the first problems that came up was whether or not to use aerial torpedo bombing. The water in Pearl Harbor was so shallow that torpedoes would probably sink to the bottom of the harbor without causing any damage. During the early months of 1941 aerial torpedo bombing was discussed, accepted, and rejected several times. Finally, it was agreed to include this kind of bombing during Operation Hawaii.

By June, Genda had developed an aerial torpedo program. He chose Kyushu Air Base on the southernmost island of Japan for the training. The area looked a little like Hawaii, and during the summer and autumn months his crews practiced aerial torpedo bombing almost every day. The results were discouraging, but Genda kept encouraging his crews.

While these practices were going on in Japan, Kimmel

received a memo dated June 13 from Washington. The memo said that recent aerial torpedo bombing tests made by the United States and Great Britain showed some success in hitting a target in water that was less than 75 feet (22.5 m) deep. The navy had always assumed aerial torpedo strikes could not be successful unless the torpedoes were dropped into water over 75 feet.

The memo told Kimmel to consider the information while planning his strategy against an enemy. He was also told to study how the new bombing results could affect his ships at Pearl Harbor. After giving a lot of thought to aerial torpedo bombing in less than 75 feet, Kimmel still believed Pearl Harbor's 40-foot (12-m) water depth was too shallow for successful bombing by an enemy.

However, the Japanese had been perfecting aerial torpedo bombing since 1933. By 1940 they had cut the depth at which torpedoes could be successful to 40 feet (12 m). When they had accomplished this, they believed they had reached perfection. Then Genda asked his bombers to cut the depth to 33 feet (10 m).

He did not tell them why they had to make the impossible possible. He only told them to succeed. The crews practiced harder than ever but were unsuccessful. In fact, there were so many failures that some of Genda's officers recommended that aerial torpedo bombing for Operation Hawaii be scrapped.

But Genda would not give up. When practices did not improve, his focus changed to improving the fins that steadied the torpedoes. By September a fin was developed that could stabilize torpedoes long enough for them to slick through shallow water instead of diving to the bottom.

The crews who made the practice runs worked incredible hours. Genda and Lieutenant Commander Mitsuo Fuchida, flight leader of the Pearl Harbor attack, wanted to tell them why they were working their crews so hard. But the fewer people who knew about Operation Hawaii, the better the chance of success. The pilots and torpedo bombers continued their long hours with no idea of what they would bomb.

While torpedo problems were being solved, Yoshikawa, Japan's spy in Hawaii, was reporting that ships at Pearl Harbor were usually anchored in pairs. When Yamamoto, Genda, and Fuchida read this information, they were disappointed. Although torpedoes could destroy the ship anchored on the outside of the pair, they would not be able to destroy the inside ship.

The inner ships would have to be destroyed with bombs dropped on their decks. It was decided that planes would bomb the ships moored on the inside of the pair with 16-inch (40-cm) shells that could go through steel. Now, in addition to torpedo practice, crews also practiced with 16-inch shells. Still they were not told why they had to work long days every day.

A Vacation in Honolulu

Through these months of work, Nagumo was saying he still did not like the odds. To get information that would give him better odds, Toshihide Maejima, Keiu Matsuo, and Suguru Suzuki sailed on the *Taiyo Maru*, a Japanese luxury ship, on October 22 for a "vacation" in Honolulu.

Maejima was an expert on large submarines, and Matsuo was an expert on midget submarines. Their orders were to learn the best way to get submarines in and around the Pearl Harbor area before the attack. Suzuki's job was to gather information on anything that would affect Japan's Operation Hawaii. The *Taiyo Maru* sailed farther north than it usually did on its luxury trips and then came south. This was the route Japan's warships would take. Passengers were never told why their vacation ship took an unusual course.

Several times a day during the cruise, Maejima, Matsuo, and Suzuki checked the weather conditions and noted how far they had traveled. They also made notes about wind direction and speed, about sea conditions and how they affected the roll of the ship. At night they took turns searching for ship lights and anything else that could jeopardize Japan's ships as they moved toward Pearl Harbor.

When the *Taiyo Maru* was 200 miles (320 km) from Hawaii, Suzuki spotted a U.S. patrol plane. At 100 miles (160 km), he saw several planes. They pretended to attack the *Taiyo Maru* and then headed back to Hawaii. Suzuki made a note that 100 miles from Hawaii was probably the attack point for U.S. planes.

For years Japanese ships, with their white flag with red rising sun, had been welcomed by hula dancers in grass skirts. The dancers put flower leis around the necks of people arriving for a vacation or to begin a new life in Hawaii. But on November 1, when the ship pulled into port, there were no hula dancers or leis for the passengers. Because of the growing problems between them, the United States and Japan had stopped trading with each other; and although Japan's passenger ships were allowed into U.S. ports, they were no longer welcomed.

When the ship anchored at Aloha Tower at 8:30 A.M., people from U.S. customs and immigration began checking papers. The customs agents examined things passengers wanted to bring ashore, and the immigration agents checked the passengers' papers. These were, and still are, normal procedures when foreigners enter U.S. ports.

But people on the *Taiyo Maru* received special attention. With the customs and immigration people there were agents from the FBI and members of U.S. Army Intelligence. The FBI and the army were looking for spies who might come in as passengers, but they did not find any. When the government people left, Suzuki and the others breathed a sigh of relief.

For the rest of the day Suzuki spent a lot of time on the bridge with a pair of binoculars. The next day he watched a peaceful Sunday morning on Oahu. He did not see any U.S. military planes flying nor any ship movement—nothing that worried him. Throughout the ship's stay, Suzuki never went ashore. He just kept checking what time planes took off, what kinds of planes they were, what direction they flew, and how long they were gone. While Suzuki did this, Maejima and Matsuo searched for the safest places for their submarines to patrol before, during, and after the attack.

Kita, the Japanese consul, visited the three men the day they docked, and he came back several times with other members of the consulate. Each time they brought military information from Yoshikawa hidden in newspapers. After they left, Suzuki often went to the bridge with his binoculars to confirm the information he had just received from the consulate's legal spies.

Suzuki wished he could talk to Yoshikawa about the information he had gathered, but a meeting might expose Yoshikawa and stop his espionage in Hawaii. So Suzuki sneaked a ball of rice paper into Kita's hand and asked him to give it to Yoshikawa. The rice paper had almost a hundred questions about the U.S. military for Yoshikawa to answer.

Yoshikawa brushed tiny characters on the rice paper and answered the questions with as few words as possible so that the answers could be smuggled aboard the *Taiyo Maru* without attracting attention. Yoshikawa checked and double-checked his information before sending it to Suzuki. He also drew maps of the ships in the harbor, of planes on airfields, of civilian airports, and even of civilian golf courses in case the U.S. military had to use them for emergency landings.

Whatever information Maejima, Matsuo, and Suzuki gathered or received was obtained while officers from U.S. customs, the FBI, naval intelligence, and army intelligence watched their ship. The *Taiyo Maru* left Hawaii on November 5 with information Yamamoto and his officers would use during the final days before Operation Hawaii.

Back in the United States

On the day the *Taiyo Maru* sailed for Honolulu with its legal spies aboard, Kimmel asked Admiral Stark for ships. Since taking command of the Pacific Fleet he constantly tried to get more ships. He asked for destroyers, cruisers, and battleships. He also asked for more long-range submarines. He did not get any. In fact, in the middle of October he lost some of the submarines he had. They left Hawaii to help defend territories in the West and South Pacific from possible attacks by Japan.

While Kimmel was losing his submarines, twenty-five large Japanese submarines and five midget submarines were ready for their part in Operation Hawaii. Because of the information supplied by Maejima and Matsuo, it had been decided that the midgets would sneak into Pearl Harbor and the large submarines would surround Hawaii.

The submarine commanders had several orders from Yamamoto. On December 6 they were to radio the latest information about the U.S. Pacific Fleet to Nagumo's ships. This would warn him if his fleet was in serious danger. It would also tell Japan's pilots which U.S. ships were in Pearl Harbor. If U.S. ships tried to leave the harbor after the attack, the submarines would destroy them. After the bombing, submarines would pick up Japanese fliers who had been shot down.

To make sure his superiors received the latest and most accurate information, Yoshikawa started dividing Pearl Harbor into sections on paper. This sectioning speeded up the reporting of U.S. ship and plane movements and made the reports easier to read.

This special interest in U.S. ships and planes by Japan was picked up by Magic. But although the people authorized to receive Magic's information knew of Japan's growing curiosity about Hawaii, Admiral Kimmel and General Short were not told.

On September 11, President Roosevelt gave a radio talk. German submarines had been attacking U.S. ships in the Atlantic, and he warned Germany that the United States would take action to protect its ships. Kimmel heard the president's speech and wrote to Stark the next day. He told Stark that the president had not said anything about Japan's interest in the Pacific, and Kimmel was worried that he might lose more ships to the Atlantic.

Again Kimmel asked that a couple of battleships be sent to Pearl Harbor. The battleships would warn the Japanese that the United States was watching them and was serious about defending the Pacific. In the same letter Kimmel asked what he should do if Japanese submarines came too close to Pearl Harbor or to his ships at sea.

Stark answered on September 23. He said the navy had no intentions of taking ships from Pearl Harbor. Then he reminded Kimmel that U.S. orders concerning Japanese submarines were not to fire at them. But if they were in or near U.S. territories, Kimmel should give a warning and then threaten U.S. action against the submarines.

Stark's letter stayed on his desk until September 29. On that day he added that Ambassador Nomura had visited him and that negotiations between Japan and the

United States were going badly. Nomura had said that relations between the two countries would grow worse if negotiations between him and Secretary of State Hull ended.

Hull, unfortunately, was fighting a losing battle and, because of Magic, he knew it. Through messages from Magic he had learned about Japan's October 15 deadline for diplomatic negotiations. He also learned from Magic that Japan would begin its Southern Operation soon after the deadline. If Japan did not get raw materials soon, it could not keep its navy and army in action.

Deadlines are always worrisome, but the October 15 deadline passed without incident. Then, on October 16, Japan's foreign minister resigned, and Emperor Hirohito appointed an army general, Hideki Tojo, as premier. In Japan the military had run the government for years, and Tojo, who came from a military background, believed in military conquest. If Hull had been concerned about a deadline on negotiations, he was doubly concerned about Tojo's appointment.

Yamamoto also worried about Tojo's appointment. He did not like Tojo. And he did not like the naval officer Tojo appointed to his cabinet. Yamamoto thought the naval officer was too weak to stand up to Tojo's demands, whatever those demands might be. Yamamoto began to worry about his Operation Hawaii.

He was not the only person worried about the new Japanese government. When President Roosevelt learned about the changes through Magic, he called for an emergency meeting with his advisers, including the secretaries of the army and the navy. The advisers felt Japan's new government would be more willing to fight the United States than the previous government had been. After the meeting Stark sent a message to Kimmel, telling him about Japan's new government and warning him to place his ships and submarines in areas where they could best protect and defend U.S. territories and those of its allies.

Kimmel jumped into action. He sent planes and submarines to Wake and Midway to run patrols around the islands. He also sent marines to reinforce troops on Johnston and Palmyra islands. Several days later Kimmel reported his actions to Stark and used the opportunity to ask for submarines, cruisers, destroyers, and the two battleships he had requested earlier. However, he got nothing since the United States—distracted by the war in Europe—was deploying more and more arms in the Atlantic.

For the same reason, General Short was not receiving what he needed, either. Like Kimmel, Short had been told about the change in Japan's cabinet and ordered to be on alert. Short continued his Alert 1, which kept his troops ready for sabotage on military installations in Hawaii.

Magic continued to pick up more and more reports that Japan would attack soon somewhere in the Pacific. To most people in the U.S. government and the military this meant the Philippine Islands. And every day that Japan did not attack was one more day the United States would have to build up its troops and equipment on the islands.

Those troops stopped in Hawaii on their way to the Philippines, and Kimmel received orders to supply planes and ships to escort them safely through the Pacific. With many of his planes and ships already patrolling U.S. territories, these new orders scattered his forces throughout the Pacific without providing reinforcements.

Meanwhile, Yamamoto was no longer worried about Premier Tojo. Japan's new leader was giving him everything he needed for Operation Hawaii.

THE FINAL COUNTDOWN

No one told Ambassador Nomura that Japan's military was preparing an attack on Hawaii. After he heard rumors around Washington about a possible attack, he believed he was being used by his government to hide its plans for war. Nomura did not want to be part of the deceit, and he suggested that he retire. But that was not allowed. Japan needed Nomura in Washington, and he was told to stay.

On October 30, Japan's government approved a list of what the United States must agree to accept before negotiations could succeed. The list was sent to Nomura and became known as Proposal A. Proposal A stated, among other things, that the United States would end its economic bans and would begin selling scrap metal and oil to Japan. Japan would stay in the Tripartite Pact with Germany and Italy, which the United States considered a move toward war. And Japan would not take its troops out of French Indochina or China.

But although Japan said it would not negotiate about French Indochina, it might negotiate about China, as long as Japan's troops could stay there for at least twenty-five years. Although Nomura did not think Secretary of State Hull would accept Proposal A, he gave it to him on

November 7. His government had ordered him to present the proposal, and he had to follow orders.

Because of Magic, Hull knew what was written on the papers before Nomura gave them to him. After he pretended to read them, he told Nomura the United States could not accept Proposal A. Nomura then asked Hull to arrange a meeting with President Roosevelt. The president had always been friendly and Nomura hoped he could get him to accept at least part of Proposal A. The president met with Nomura on November 10, but he agreed with Secretary Hull that the United States could not accept any part of the proposal.

On November 13, Nomura sent a cable to Japan's foreign minister, Shigenori Togo. Nomura said that, despite the fact that the United States wanted Japan's troops out of Indochina and China, he would try again to persuade Secretary of State Hull and President Roosevelt to accept Proposal A. Nomura asked Togo to be patient, but Togo refused. He decided he needed a stronger ambassador to work with Nomura. Saburo Kurusu arrived in Washington on November 15, the day before Japan's submarines headed for Hawaii.

On November 20, Kurusu was with Nomura when he gave Hull Japan's Proposal B. Proposal B was almost the same as Proposal A, and Nomura knew the U.S. government would turn it down as quickly as it had turned down Proposal A. But Togo told him negotiations had to continue no matter how Nomura or the United States felt about the proposals.

Not only did Nomura have proposals the United States would not accept, he also had a November 25 deadline for their acceptance. Nomura wondered why he had to get an agreement signed by that date. What he did not know was that on November 26 (in Japan, which would be November 25 in the United States) Japan's First

Fleet would head across the North Pacific to attack Hawaii. If the United States signed an agreement by November 25, the fleet would not leave Japan. Togo knew there was little chance that the United States would sign the proposals. He was using them to play for time.

Secretary of State Hull was also playing for time. On November 26 he and his advisers wrote what became known as the Ten-Point Memorandum. The memo said, among other things, that the United States would try to work out an acceptable trade agreement with Japan, which was one of the things Japan had asked for during negotiations. But it also said that if Japan wanted to establish friendly relations it would have to take its troops out of Indochina and China. Just as Nomura did not believe the United States would accept proposals A or B, Hull did not believe Japan would accept his memo. But the memo would give the United States more time to prepare for the war he knew was coming.

After Togo read Hull's Ten-Point Memorandum, he told reporters that while Japan was negotiating with the United States for peace Secretary Hull had sent Japan an ultimatum for war. While Togo was complaining to the press, Japan's submarines and ships were sailing toward Hawaii. Japan also had ships moving through the West and South Pacific to be ready to attack the Philippines, Guam, Wake, Midway, Malaya, and Hong Kong.

As Hull and Togo played for time, Captain Mayfield finally found a way to get copies of the Japanese consulate cablegrams. When David Sarnoff, the president of the Radio Corporation of America visited Hawaii, Mayfield asked him to help his Intelligence Office get copies of the consulate's messages. Although it was against the law, Sarnoff agreed to help Mayfield.

Unfortunately, the Japanese consulate always sent its messages through RCA one month and through MacKay

Radio the next month. During November their messages went out over the MacKay Radio wires, and Mayfield did not get any information. But in December RCA gave him the copies he wanted. He turned them over to Commander Joseph J. Rochefort, head of the Naval Intelligence Unit at Pearl Harbor, who gave them top priority. But although his people worked sixteen hours a day, they did not get all of the messages decoded and translated until December 10. The messages were filled with information that would have alerted the United States of the Japanese attack on Pearl Harbor.

U.S. War Warnings

On November 24, Stark sent a message to Kimmel. He said that with negotiations breaking down and Japan's ships on the move, it seemed as though Japan was planning a surprise attack somewhere in the Pacific. He also said that the Philippines and Guam were possible targets. Kimmel showed the message to Short. Since there was no mention of Hawaii, neither man ordered any change in the defense of the ships or the islands.

On November 27, Stark sent another message to Kimmel. The first sentence told Kimmel the message was a war warning: an "aggressive move" by Japan was expected in a few days. And the large number of Japanese troops and ships seemed to indicate an attack against the Philippines, Borneo, or the Thai or Kra peninsula.

The "war warning" phrase had never been used in messages to Kimmel, and Stark expected him to take the words seriously. But since the message did not say an attack on Hawaii was imminent, Kimmel did nothing. He had already received several warnings of possible attacks by Japan. To him the war warning was just a repetition of what had already been said in other messages. Since he had been training his crews for months on how to defend their ships, there was no reason to change his current orders, which were to defend his ships at sea, not in his own backyard.

General Short also read the "war message" and, like Kimmel, did not think Japan would attack Hawaii. But he believed they would sabotage equipment, especially his planes. After discussions with his officers, Short decided to keep the islands on Alert 1. Then he sent a message to his superiors in Washington telling them of his decision. Since they did not question what he had done, he felt he had made the right decision.

Kimmel and Short met several times between November 27 and December 7, but their plans for the defense of Hawaii hardly changed. Kimmel continued to believe the army was on Alert 2, ready to defend his ships in the harbor. And Short continued to believe the navy was patrolling the areas around Hawaii.

Japan's First Fleet Under Way

While Kimmel and Short were receiving war messages from their superiors, Japan's First Fleet sailed out of the harbor at Hitokappu Bay in the Kurile Islands. The sea pounded against the ships, fog surrounded them, and gales blew across their decks. Everything Nagumo had feared about the weather was happening. During the next few days the wind and sea continued to worry him.

Three days after the ships left the harbor some of them had to be refueled. Refueling was another thing Nagumo had worried about, and he had reason to worry. As the ships rose and fell in the heavy seas, some of the hoses hooked between the ships and the oil tankers broke loose and crashed across the decks. Some sailors were swept overboard, but despite the danger the refueling continued.

After this first refueling the fog often cleared and the winds and seas calmed. But Nagumo could not relax. Now he worried that if the sky stayed cloudless and the sea remained calm, his ships could be seen for miles in all directions. If an enemy spotted them, his name would appear in history books as the man who lost most of Japan's naval air strength in a few minutes.

As days passed, his crews became more and more restless. Pilots checked and rechecked their planes. They started engines. They wondered what and where they would bomb. Everyone had orders to watch for ships and planes. The task force was always blacked out, and their radios were silent. Sailors and pilots bet on their destination. And Nagumo had trouble sleeping.

While Nagumo worried, on December 2 (in Japan) an Imperial Conference was held at the emperor's palace. Premier Hideki Tojo and Foreign Minister Shigenori Togo were there. So were Admiral Yamamoto and other officers. Most of the meeting was spent talking about the need for war with the United States.

While the talk of war went on and on, Emperor Hirohito sat silent. In September when talk of war had come up, the emperor had insisted that Japan and the United States solve their problems with negotiation, not war. But now those in the room accepted the emperor's silence as approval for Operation Hawaii.

Having agreed on war, Yamamoto said that an attack without warning was against the code of honor among nations. He had believed Operation Hawaii must be a surprise, but now he said the United States should receive a warning that Japan was going to attack. Others believed that if there were no surprise Japan stood to lose too many ships, planes, and people.

After more discussions they agreed that the United States would be told diplomatic negotiations would end at

1:30 P.M. on Sunday, December 7, Washington time. Since the attack was planned for 8 A.M. in Hawaii, this would give the United States a half hour warning. After the meeting ended, Nagumo received a message. Now that the emperor had tacitly agreed to war, Nagumo was given permission to tell his men that their target was Hawaii.

They cheered when they heard the news. Since their destination was no longer a secret, relief maps of Pearl Harbor were hung on the hangar decks for the crews to study. Pearl Harbor, Hickam, Wheeler, Schofield were all there, and pilots studied them over and over again. While the men crammed their heads with information, Nagumo kept worrying that his ships would be spotted.

If they were spotted before December 6, he had orders to return to Japan. If they were spotted on the 6th, he was to make his own decision about whether to carry out Operation Hawaii or go back to Japan. If they were spotted on the 7th, he was to attack. On December 3 the ships crossed the international date line. Now they were on the same date as the United States. (Travelers crossing the international date line in the Pacific change dates, subtracting one day if heading east and adding one day when going west.)

Creating Confusion

While the First Air Fleet moved closer and closer to Hawaii, Japan tried to confuse U.S. intelligence. It succeeded. One of the things Japan's navy did was to bring busloads of sailors into Tokyo from their barracks and take them on sight-seeing tours on December 5, 6, and 7. This was supposed to fool U.S. intelligence into believing Japan had no planned military action. If an attack was planned, hundreds of sailors would not be crowding into Tokyo on leave. The deception worked long enough to be helpful.

Japan also sent false messages over its radios to hide the movement of Nagumo's fleet. On December 1, Japan's navy changed its code for the second time in a month. This worried Commander Rochefort in the U.S. Intelligence Office. When a country changed codes that often, it usually meant the country was ready to declare war. And the code changes meant Rochefort could no longer keep track of Japan's ships. He knew some of them were moving west and south. Japan did not seem to be trying to hide those ships. But he did not know where the rest of the fleet was. The ships seemed to have disappeared from the face of the earth.

Togo's Orders

On December 1, Togo told Nomura that the consulate offices in London, Hong Kong, Singapore, and Manila had been ordered to destroy their code machines. And when the time came for Nomura to get rid of his machines, he was to ask Japan's naval office in Washington to help him. Workers there could do the job quickly.

On December 4, Nomura was told to destroy secret papers. On the 5th, Japan's officials were told to get ready to leave the United States. On the 6th, Togo told Nomura he would be receiving a fourteen-part message in answer to Hull's Ten-Point Memorandum. The message would also tell him when to give the answer to Hull. All of this was picked up by Magic. And everyone authorized to read Magic's messages tried to figure out when and where Japan would attack.

With war moving closer and closer, President Roosevelt wrote to Emperor Hirohito on the afternoon of December 6. The letter began with a reminder of the long peace and friendship between their two countries and asked for these to continue. The letter did not reach the emperor until after the attack on Pearl Harbor; but even if it had reached him, it was too late to stop the bombing.

While President Roosevelt was writing to Emperor Hirohito, Yoshikawa, Japan's spy in Hawaii, was still sending information about U.S. ships. On the evening of December 6, Denise Smith was working at her desk at RCA before going to a party with her husband. Before she left the office, she handled a coded message from the Japanese consulate. It was the last one Yoshikawa sent.

From November 19 to December 6, Yoshikawa sent twenty-four radiograms to Yamamoto, who sent all of Yoshikawa's information to Nagumo. On December 6, when Yamamoto gave the last message to Nagumo, he added, "The moment has arrived. The rise or fall of our Empire is at stake." Nagumo did not sleep much that night. Neither did his officers and their crews.

In Washington, President Roosevelt was also receiving messages on the evening of the 6th. U.S. intelligence sent about fifteen typed pages to the White House. These pages contained thirteen parts of the fourteen-part message Togo told Nomura he would send. One of the things the president read was that Japan was rejecting Hull's Ten-Point Memorandum. When the president finished reading, he told Harry Hopkins, his friend and adviser, that the message meant war. Hopkins agreed and hinted that the United States should attack first and surprise Japan. But the president believed that one country did not attack another without first declaring war.

Shortly before midnight the president talked with Admiral Stark about the thirteen parts of Togo's message. Because Stark had read many messages U.S. intelligence had intercepted, he decided that this one was a repetition of what he already knew. His reaction was similar to Kimmel's and Short's reactions to their messages from

Washington. It was as though people had cried wolf so often it was hard to believe that this warning was real.

The fourteenth part of the message did not come in until the early morning of December 7. This was not an accident; Togo had planned it that way. He did not send the thirteen parts of the message in order. He also did not send them all at once. And then he told Nomura that the message was too secret to give to a typist to prepare for Hull. Nomura found only one official in his consulate who could satisfy Togo's demands for secrecy. And that person could hardly type. Since the message was several pages long and had to be decoded and put in a presentable form, Togo's instructions were almost impossible to carry out.

U.S. intelligence had the fourteenth part of the message ready for President Roosevelt to read at around 10 A.M. on the 7th. It ended: "The Japanese Government regrets to have to notify hereby the American Government that in view of the attitude of the American Government it cannot but consider that it is impossible to reach an agreement through further negotiations."

Nomura had been told to deliver the message to Hull at 1 P.M., with negotiations to end at 1:30. That would be 7:30 A.M. in Hawaii. This was the thirty-minute declaration of war warning agreed on at the Imperial Conference. But because of the restrictions about secrecy that Togo put on Nomura, the message was not ready to present to Hull until after 2:00. Therefore, the United States did not receive an official declaration of war from Japan.

General Marshall read the fourteenth part of the message at 11:25, Washington time, just as Japanese planes were taking off from their carriers to head for Pearl Harbor. Marshall and his officers agreed that the words in the fourteenth part of the message meant the Japanese would attack an American military base in the Pacific soon. They decided to warn military bases in Panama, the Philippines, Hawaii, and the west coast of the United States. That was the message General Short and Admiral Kimmel received several hours after the attack on Pearl Harbor.

By then the name Pearl Harbor had become part of history.

THE DAYS AFTER

On December 8 someone wrote on a blackboard in the CinCPAC office: "Your conduct and action have been splendid. We took a blow yesterday. It will not be a short war. We will give many blows to the Japanese. Carry on. Keep smiling."

Although people did not smile much, they carried on. In Hawaii rescue operations continued. In the United States, when recruiting stations opened on December 8, people were lined up, ready to join the navy, army, marines, or Coast Guard. Some had been there all night.

Neighbors helped neighbors cope with the worry about loved ones who were in Hawaii. Were they all right? Were they hurt? Were they dead? In 1941 there were no instant television broadcasts of events happening thousands of miles away. And with the islands under martial law it was hard for people in Hawaii to call home and let families and friends know they were safe. When someone got a call through, it was limited and censored. Phone lines had to be kept open for official business. The country was at war.

In many cases it took weeks to learn if relatives or friends were alive or dead. Families of the dead and wounded were notified privately by the government. But the government made mistakes. People were reported dead who, after the confusion of the first few days, were found to be alive. Stories like this gave some families and friends false hope. When they were told a loved one was dead, many hoped the government had made another mistake. Unfortunately, most of the time the government was right.

Newspapers and radio news broadcasts did not give the real numbers of dead and wounded or how many ships and planes had been destroyed. This was partly because the government was still gathering information about what had happened. It was also to protect Americans from the real number of casualties in Hawaii. The reasoning was similar to the order given on the day of the attack that bodies should be moved to the collection area at night when fewer people would be on the streets. People could handle only a certain amount of bad news.

But the idea of not releasing figures was not only for the emotional health of the country. It was also to prevent Japan and Germany from learning the extent of the damage in Pearl Harbor. Now that the countries were at war, nothing should be said or done that would put the U.S. military in danger.

Americans went from sorrow to anger and back to sorrow and anger until the two emotions blended. They were angry at Japan, but many were also angry with the U.S. government and the politicians who ran it. How could they have been so surprised? They should have known Japan was planning an attack. How could thirty ships sneak through thousands of miles of ocean without being seen? People coped with their anger in different ways. One man cut down four of the Japanese trees in Washington's Potomac Park. Two of the four were original trees given to the United States by Japan when the countries were friends.

During the time the United States was selling scrap

metal and oil to Japan, many people had said that someday those materials would be used against the United States. The attack on Pearl Harbor proved them right. But this was not a time to gloat about being right. This was a time to join together and fight. Japan had attacked U.S. soil without a declaration of war—a criminal act—and Japan had to be punished.

Despite the sorrow and the anger, some people felt relief. War in Europe and the sinking of American ships by Germany had threatened the United States for months. When the United States declared war against Germany and Italy on December 11, Americans felt their country could get on with the job of saving the world from its enemies. But even people who felt relief at being able to fight wanted to know the facts about Pearl Harbor.

On December 9, Secretary of the Navy Frank Knox went to Hawaii to try to learn why Japan was able to attack with such surprise and success. When Knox asked Kimmel and Short this question, they admitted they had not expected an air attack on Hawaii. When questioned further, Kimmel told Knox he had thought that if Japan attacked Hawaii it would be with submarines. Short said he believed Japan would do its damage on the islands by sabotaging equipment.

Knox was surprised by their answers and shocked by what he saw in and around Pearl Harbor. The Pacific Fleet was in shambles. Burned planes, hangars, and equipment were everywhere. But the human loss and suffering hit Knox the hardest.

At Hospital Point he saw hundreds of people burned beyond recognition. Some were so charred that their skin was black and oozing. Tubes hung from their arms to drain poisons from their burns. Knox watched bodies being taken from the oil-covered water. The bodies washed ashore or bobbed up, bloated from being in the water so long. The people removing the bodies looked as though they had not slept since the first bomb fell. Some had only catnapped. But they kept pulling bodies from the water and praying to find survivors.

Knox returned to the United States on December 14. He went to the White House to talk to President Roosevelt and give him casualty lists and pictures of the damage to military areas. After Knox left, the president was so depressed by what he had been told that his aides worried about his health.

Americans Pitch In

To help win the war people poured into Washington to work in government offices. Many offices stayed open twenty-four hours a day and on weekends and holidays. Manufacturers hired thousands of workers throughout the United States. After ten years of high unemployment caused by the depression of the 1930s, people were willing to work anywhere, anytime, and to do anything to help themselves and their country.

Over time Americans responded to the reality of war. War bonds and stamps went on sale, and people bought them with dimes and dollars. Drives to collect scrap metal, fats, rubber, anything that would help defeat their enemies were organized. The Capitol dome was blacked out. So were homes. Windows were covered with curtains, shades, or black paint. Block wardens patrolled neighborhoods at night to make sure no light showed from any of the houses on their blocks. Schoolchildren practiced air raid drills. People who lived on the east and west coasts talked about moving to the center of the country. Gas, tires, and foods were rationed. Some people hoarded things; some even sold rationed items for prices much higher than they were worth. But most people banded together to defeat their enemies.

Japanese Heroes
for the United States

When Japan attacked Hawaii, there were about 160,000 Japanese living on the islands. As soon as the bombs started falling, rumors against the Japanese population began: They would kill anyone who tried to stop them; they would help the invading Japanese take over the island. There was one rumor that a Japanese laborer had cut arrows in sugarcane fields to show the attacking planes the way to Pearl Harbor. All of the rumors were checked out; none was true.

Even the Japanese who were American citizens were suspected of being spies and saboteurs. But the Japanese in Hawaii stayed loyal to the United States, and many served in the U.S. military. The army's 442nd Regimental Combat Team, made up mostly of second-generation Americans of Japanese ancestry fought in Europe and became one of the most decorated regiments of World War II. Also, hundreds of Japanese helped the United States by working as interpreters and translators in the Pacific area.

Retirements and Investigations

On December 16, Kimmel and Short were relieved of their duties for not being prepared on December 7. On the 17th they turned over their commands to their replacements. That same day a group appointed by the government met in Washington to investigate who was responsible for the losses in Hawaii. This group was called the Roberts Commission.

On January 24, 1942, the Roberts Commission gave its report to President Roosevelt. Most of the blame was placed on Kimmel and Short. The commission concluded that their errors in judgment were responsible for Japan's success. Short and Kimmel were given the opportunity to take early retirement instead of being forced out, and they did so. General Short's retirement began on February 28; Admiral Kimmel's, on March 1. Both men were embarrassed and angry and felt they had been treated unfairly.

The Roberts Commission was the first to investigate what happened in Hawaii. There would be seven more investigations. The last one, by a Joint Congressional Committee, began in September 1945 and ended in July 1946. It also concluded that Kimmel and Short had made "errors in judgment." For the rest of their lives the two officers lived with those words on their military records. Admiral Husband E. Kimmel died on May 14, 1968. General Walter C. Short died September 3, 1949.

For the Japanese who carried out Operation Hawaii, there were no investigations, only admiration and praise from their government. But many of these men died fighting in the war they had started. Admiral Isoroku Yamamoto, who thought up Operation Hawaii, was shot down by American flyers over the Solomon Islands on April 18, 1943. Admiral Chichi Nagumo, whose carriers brought the attack planes within 200 miles (320 km) of Hawaii, died during the summer of 1944 when U.S. forces invaded the Marianas. And Petty Officer Noboru Kanai, who was credited with dropping the bomb that caused the *Arizona* to blow up, was shot down by American flyers during Japan's attack on Wake Island. But Commander Mitsuo Fuchida and Commander Minoru Genda survived the war. Fuchida was on board the USS *Missouri* when Japan surrendered to the United States on September 2, 1945. Genda lived to serve four terms as a member of the Diet, Japan's parliament.

The USS *Arizona* Memorial

One thousand one hundred seventy-seven sailors and marines died on the *Arizona* when it blew up on December 7, including Rear Admiral Isaac Kidd, commander of the First Battleship Division. His body was never recovered, but his naval academy class ring was found embedded in the *Arizona's* steel tower by a salvage crew. The crew also found the admiral's uniforms and his sword. Thirty years later these were discovered in a crate in his widow's basement. Also in the crate was a plaque from the *Arizona*. The plaque was sent to Hawaii, where it is a part of the USS *Arizona* Memorial.

The salvage work on the *Arizona* ended in the summer of 1942. The crews recovered two of the ship's bells. One of them is now displayed in the entry room of the memorial. Also salvaged were guns and equipment, which were used to repair and equip other ships that fought in the Pacific during the war. When the salvage work ended, the navy's Bureau of Ships gathered information to find out why the *Arizona* blew up when other ships in Pearl Harbor did not.

In 1944, using reports from salvage crews and a film that showed where the Japanese bombs hit and the ship's position when it went down, the bureau determined that the explosion probably happened when a hatch on the third deck of the ship was left open. A bomb went through the hatch and down the passageway to the ship's ceremonial ammunition area. The bureau concluded that the heat from the burning ammunition started fires that moments later reached the six ammunition magazines in the forward part of the ship.

The hulk of the *Arizona* became an unofficial memorial to the sailors and marines killed on December 7, and ships saluted it as they passed. In 1950 a flagpole was raised on the hulk of the battleship, and on Memorial Day 1962 a permanent memorial in the form of a bridge spanning the hulk of the *Arizona* was dedicated. The remains of the battleship rest in 38 feet (11.3 m) of water at the bottom of Pearl Harbor. The more than 1.5 million people who come to the memorial every year can see the remains from the concrete bridge. They can also see the oil that still seeps from the *Arizona*. Parts of its mainmast and the rusted shield for its third gun turret are all that protrude above the water.

The names of the men who died on the *Arizona* are inscribed on a white marble wall in a shrine at the memorial, which is dedicated to all of the people who died at Pearl Harbor. In 1980 it became part of the U.S. National Park Service, and a visitor's center was built.

The remains of the *Arizona* are covered with sea life, including barnacles, corals, sponges, and grasses. It does not look at all like the *Arizona* that was moored in Pearl Harbor on December 7, 1941. But the visitors who come from all over the world recall a day of infamy when they look down at the ghost of the *Arizona* and read the memorial plaque:

Dedicated to the Eternal Memory
of Our Gallant Shipmates in the USS Arizona
Who Gave Their Lives in Action
7 December 1941

EPILOGUE

On December 7, 1941, the United States military warning system in the Pacific should have protected Pearl Harbor from an extensive loss of people, ships, and planes, but it failed. It failed because no one expected the Japanese to attack American bases in Hawaii. For example, when it worked, the newly installed Opana Mobile Radar Station was usually turned on between 4 and 7 in the morning. On December 7, the station actually picked up blips from the invading Japanese planes, but no one realized what the blips signified, so no warning was passed along the chain of command.

When World War II ended in 1945, the United States government decided to abandon isolationism and became an active member of the world community. More importantly, it was determined to prevent sneak attacks like Pearl Harbor from ever happening again. The stakes were even higher. During the war, a new weapon, the atomic bomb, and a new delivery system, the V-2 rocket, were developed that would make such attacks far more devastating. In August 1945, the United States dropped atomic bombs on the Japanese cities of Hiroshima and Nagasaki. The Nazi Germans used V-2 rockets to bomb Great Britain. After the war, more sophisticated versions of these devices were perfected, and the two most powerful nations in the world—the United States and the Soviet Union— found themselves propelled into a race for military supremacy that continued for decades.

Modern delivery systems and weapons are light-years away from the devices used during World War II. The United States and the Soviet Union developed Intermediate Range Ballistic Missiles (IRBMs) and Intercontinental Ballistic Missiles (ICBMs), capable of delivering nuclear warheads over great distances. These warheads are over five hundred times more powerful than the atomic bomb dropped on Hiroshima, which exploded with a force equivalent to 15,000 tons of TNT. Today, cruise missiles can travel 1,500 miles (2,400 km), while a torpedo fired by a World War II submarine could only travel about 6 miles (9.6 km).

Shortly after World War II, discussions began on how to protect the United States against surprise attacks. By 1952, the United States military agreed that it needed a warning system. In cooperation with Canada, a sophisticated radar system known as the Defense Early Warning System was erected across the North Pole, the shortest distance between the United States and the Soviet Union. The Dew Line, as it was soon called, ran from Point Barrow, Alaska, to the eastern shore of Canada's Baffin Island. This radar shield was built through the Arctic Circle, where high winds often reach 100 miles (161 km) an hour and the temperature could fall to 80 degrees below zero (27 degrees C). The shield would be able to pick up the presence of approaching aircraft, and eventually, missiles.

Unlike the primitive type of radar used in Hawaii on December 7, 1941, the Dew Line is a twenty-four-hour alert system that sends signals to the Continental Air Defense (CONAD) station located in the Combat Operations Defense Center in Colorado Springs, Colorado. The people at CONAD decode signals from the radar shield to learn what kinds of aircraft are approaching, their altitude, and the direction in which they are flying. CONAD determines whether the incoming aircraft pose a threat to North America.

Although the Dew Line is 3,000 miles (4,800 km) long, it is only a part of the 10,000-mile (16,000-km) circle comprised of radar-equipped U.S. submarines, ships, and planes stationed in different areas of the world. Included in this web are nuclear-powered hunter-killer submarines, aircraft carriers, Phantom fighters, tanker planes that can refuel bombers in the air, and fighter planes that can deliver machine guns, cannons, rockets, guided missiles, and bombs. To these have been added surveillance planes, first the U-2 and now the Airborne Warning and Communication System (AWACS), and spy satellites that photograph military installations and troop movements all over the world.

An awareness of the destructive capacity of modern weapons combined with the effectiveness of early warning systems has produced a half century of peace. In the 1960s, a hot line was installed, linking the United States and the Soviet Union, to prevent misunderstandings that could accidentally trigger a nuclear war. Now the two nations are reducing their nuclear stockpiles and short-range delivery systems. However, even as the arms race winds down, Americans remember Pearl Harbor. Whatever the future brings, they are determined to be prepared.

HIGHLIGHTS OF THE ATTACK
ON PEARL HARBOR

PHOTOGRAPHY CREDITS

A NOTE ABOUT SOURCES

BIBLIOGRAPHY

INDEX

HIGHLIGHTS OF THE ATTACK ON PEARL HARBOR

1853

Commodore Matthew C. Perry arrives in Tokyo Bay.

1854

Japan signs trade treaty with United States.

1898

The United States annexes the Republic of Hawaii.

1922

The United States and Japan agree to limit naval strength.

1936

Japan renounces the 1922 agreement to limit naval strength.

1937

Japan invades China. The American ship *Panay* sunk, with loss of American lives.

1939

Germany conquers Poland. Great Britain and France declare war on Germany.

1940

May—Hawaii becomes home to the U.S. Pacific Fleet.

August—U.S. Signal Service breaks Japan's diplomatic codes.

September—Japan invades parts of Indochina.

September—The United States stops selling all raw materials to Japan except oil.

September—Japan signs the Tripartite Treaty with Germany and Italy.

December—Admiral Isoroku Yamamoto, commander in chief of Japan's navy, talks about a surprise attack on Pearl Harbor to a few of his officers.

1941

January—Ambassador Kichisaburo Nomura leaves for the United States.

February—Admiral Husband E. Kimmel becomes commander of the U.S. Pacific Fleet.

February—General Walter C. Short becomes commander of the Hawaiian Department.

March—Spy Takeo Yoshikawa arrives in Hawaii.

April—Japan reorganizes its ships into one fleet and calls it the First Air Fleet.

July—Japan occupies the rest of Indochina.

August—The United States stops selling gasoline and oil to Japan.

September—Japan's yearly war games begin in Tokyo.

November—Ambassador Nomura and special envoy Saburo Kurusu begin final negotiations with U.S. Secretary of State Cordell Hull.

November—Japan's First Fleet leaves Japan and heads for Hawaii.

November—Hull writes his Ten-Point Memorandum.

December 4—Nomura is told to destroy secret papers.

December 6—President Roosevelt writes to Emperor Hirohito and asks him to prevent war.

December 6—Last message is sent to Japan by spy Yoshikawa.

December 6—The first parts of the fourteen-part message arrive at U.S. Intelligence Office.

December 7—Final part of fourteen-part message arrives at U.S. Intelligence Office.

December 7—Japanese attack Pearl Harbor, the Philippines, Wake, Guam, Midway, Hong Kong, Malaya, and Thailand.

PHOTOGRAPHY CREDITS

Maps and photographs courtesy of: Vantage Art: pp. 1, 2; UPI/Bettmann Newsphotos: pp. 3 top, 5, 7, 9, 10 top right and bottom, 11 top, 12 top, 13 top, 14, 15 bottom, 16 bottom; AP/Wide World Photos: pp. 3 bottom, 8 bottom, 13 bottom; The Bettmann Archive: pp. 4, 6, 8 top, 11 bottom, 12 bottom, 15 top; New York Public Library, Picture Collection: p. 10 top left; National Archives: p. 16 top.

A NOTE ABOUT SOURCES

Although the author read many books while research-
ing and writing *Pearl Harbor*, Gordon W. Prange's book *At
Dawn We Slept* was used to substantiate and confirm almost all of the information in this book.

BIBLIOGRAPHY

Bliven, Bruce, Jr. *From Pearl Harbor to Okinawa.* New York: Random House, 1960.

Collier, Richard. *The Road to Pearl Harbor.* New York: Atheneum, 1981.

Grew, Joseph C. *Ten Years in Japan.* New York: Arno Press, 1972.

Hoehling, A. A. *The Week before Pearl Harbor.* New York: Norton, 1963.

Hull, Cordell. *The Memoirs of Cordell Hull.* New York: Macmillan, 1948.

Kimmel, Husband E. *Admiral Kimmel's Story.* Chicago: Regnery, 1955.

Lord, Walter. *Day of Infamy.* New York: Holt, 1957.

Prange, Gordon W. *At Dawn We Slept: The Untold Story of Pearl Harbor.* New York: Penguin Books, 1982.

———. *December 7, 1941: The Day the Japanese Attacked Pearl Harbor.* New York: McGraw-Hill, 1988.

———. *Verdict of History.* New York: McGraw-Hill, 1986.

Shapiro, William E. *Turning Points of World War II.* New York: Franklin Watts, 1984.

Skipper, E. C. *Pearl Harbor.* Chicago: Children's Press, 1983.

Taylor, Theodore. *Air Raid—Pearl Harbor!* New York: Harper & Row, 1971.

INDEX

E C I A Chapter 2

E C I A Chapter 2

ECIA Chapter 2

940.54
Dun

DUNNAHOO, TERRY
Pearl Harbor.

ECIA Chapter 2